Chris is a true story based on several years of gathering facts, official documents and eye witness accounts. It is a wonderfully entertaining story of a remarkable woman who grew up in the Great Depression, overcame multiple hardships and setbacks, defied stereotyping and demolished gender bias. She became a tender, tough, humble, brave, multi-talented, successful mother, career woman and community service volunteer and care-giver. She was the subject of several news stories during her lifetime and was widely admired and respected by men and women alike. *Ed.*

What others say about *CHRIS:*

"It was an honor to review a manuscript as well written as *Chris*. It held my attention from the first page to the last. I truly enjoyed this book! The writer has a gift for writing in the conversational voice."

— *Melanie Stiles, author and editor*

"It has been an adventure and a privilege to read *Chris*. It is a wonderful, unforgettable story. The writer's lens-like ability to zoom into the most intimate scenes and bring them to life with authenticity is remarkable. The narrative serves up humor, sadness, fear, love and mischief, against a backdrop of historical and cultural change."

— *Suzanne Underwood Rhodes, author and critic*

"With vivid and conversational writing style, Chris leaps off the pages of the book and into your heart. She is the stoic personification of a different era — a time when America was brought to her knees but never stood taller. Payne's writing takes you there and, despite the hardships, makes you yearn to live in a time like that.

Chris was a remarkable woman, worthy of a mesmerizing tale well told, and this book does her justice.

– Randy Singer, author and attorney

"Chris comes to life . . . her personality jump off the pages."
– Joey W. Melano, M.A., Stage & Screen
Production,
Regent University

"I can hardly wait for *Chris* to be published. When I read the draft, the grandmother I always loved came back to life, and I came to understand and admire her even more for the amazing lady she really was."

– Mark Payne, Ex-Marine

CHRIS

By

Charles E. Payne

First Printing: 2017
ISBN 13 9781544025865
ISBN 10 1544025866

Cover Photo, Chris at age 19
Cover Design, Gene Payne, photolithographic and portraitist

IMPORTANT INFORMATION

CHRIS was written to bring to life the woman herself, her family and the tumultuous times which shaped her destiny. All events depicted in this story actually happened. Almost all are based on personal accounts of those who were there. Where there was no living witness, historical research and known surrounding facts provided the basis for determining the details of an event. The characters are all real, though some names were changed for privacy. Whenever possible, quoted statements are as remembered. Where the actual words of a conversation were not known, dialogue was composed to reflect the mood and substance of the conversation concerning known events. *CHRIS*, therefore, is a highly factual story set in its historical context, and told as drama seasoned with a tablespoon of conjecture to bring out the flavors of ingredients in the soup.

Special thanks and appreciation go to Ms. Cathy Allen, Deputy Clerk of Fluvanna County Circuit Court, Ms. Danna Catlett of Fluvanna Baptist Church, and Ms. Stephanie Robinson of the Virginia Division of Vital Records. These ladies graciously and patiently located and provided copies of old records of people, places and events lost in the mist of years long past. My special thanks also go to my children who urged me to write this book, my wife, Carolyn, for her patience and support extending over the three years it took to research and write *Chris,* and to my brother Gene who provided memories and old photos, designed the cover of this book and provided his ready support any time I asked him.

TABLE OF CONTENTS

CHAPTER 1
A NEW WAY DAWNING

B uffalo Bill Cody was in show business staging pretend battles between real cowboys and Indians. Wyatt Earp was considering moving to Hollywood and giving advice to movie actors about how things really were back in the day. His friend Bat Masterson was a reporter in New York City writing a byline column for the *New York Morning Telegraph.* All the celebrity outlaws were dead or in prison. The Wild West was banished from the land, sentenced to spend eternity in books and movies, a phantom of what once had been.

The Industrial Age was rolling across the country on wheels and gears forged of iron. With it came the rise of cities, transforming the 46 United States. Thomas Jefferson's vision of an ennobled pastoral society was losing out to Alexander Hamilton's prophetic and pragmatic vision of an industrial one.

Mills, factories, railroads, banks, shops, stores, restaurants, hotels and steamships filled with goods from Europe and Asia offered anything a family needed or wanted, and it was all so conveniently available. So were the jobs; steady jobs and, for many, a rising standard of living. A man was no longer at the mercy and whim of nature for a successful crop or a healthy herd to support his family.

As the cornucopia of urban jobs grew, so did the stream of people leaving the family farm to fill them. Like Dorothy setting out for the Emerald City, they came seeking all that the cities promised. Opportunity was unlimited, optimism flourished, and a burgeoning middle class was beginning to write its chapter in the American story.

For only twelve hours a day, six days a week, with Sundays off, a working man in the city could buy more than just the basics. Most married women did not work outside the home. A wife's job was to run the house, take care of her husband, birth and raise their children and manage their social life. Not that a woman couldn't work outside the home. Many did by necessity. It just had to be suitable woman's work: restaurant waitress, seamstress, nurse, hair dresser, secretary, school teacher, librarian, store clerk, housekeeper, cook, laundress and such.

Corsets, bustles and outsized hats gave way to smaller hats and dresses made of lighter fabrics, with natural curves and softer lines. Something called "slacks" were popular among daring woman who had discretionary money to spend. Modern, low-top shoes were gaining popularity as paved streets and sidewalks relegated boots to inclement weather wear.

Fashionable city gentlemen wore pants and vest, a long-sleeved shirt and either a bow or fore-in-hand tie. For dressier occasions a jacket was added, three to four buttons, flap-pockets, medium to short lapels, finger-tip to mid-thigh length and a single vent. A white shirt and tie, bishop-like starched collar and fedora or bowler hat completed a gentleman's attire. The leading edge of modern clothing fashion was arriving.

The Model-T Ford was introduced in 1908. It was so cheap, rugged and reliable that the average working man could afford one. The 1910 Census pegged the US population at 96.85 million, a sizable market for cars.

Henry Ford, in a stroke of enlightened self-interest, figured out that if he paid his auto workers a higher wage they could afford to buy the cars they built. More cars bought meant more cars built, which meant more jobs, higher pay, more profit, more cars built – and the cycle spiraled upward. Ford introduced the 40-hour work week, and the hourly wage he paid was so generous that on one occasion, when a higher pay scale was announced, a riot erupted among applicants at Ford's employment office.

By 1911, the Model-T was overwhelming all other automakers and quickly filling the streets and country roads. Other car makers soon had to follow Ford's lead, all of which pushed the growth of the middle class into high gear.

In 1911, William Howard Taft had been President for only a few months. He was hand-picked to succeed Teddy Roosevelt, who kept his promise to serve only one term. Taft promised to carry on Teddy's programs to improve the pay and working conditions of the average American wage earner. That same year, Matthew Browning's first semi-automatic pistol was adopted by the US military. Dubbed the Model M-1911, it became the benchmark for pistols for the next 100 years.

In 1911, the Phillies and Giants won their league pennants and played each other in the World Series. A young Native American named Jim Thorpe, playing football for Carlisle College, almost single-handedly defeated No. 1-ranked Harvard to win the 1911 national college football title.

Also in 1911, the United States Supreme Court upheld a verdict ordering John D. Rockefeller's corporate giant, Standard Oil Company, to be broken into six separate companies. It was a happy day for Teddy and Taft, who were bent on breaking the monopolistic grip of big business on the American economy. Breaking up Standard Oil turned into a boon for Rockefeller, making him richer than he already was.

Meanwhile in 1911, boys labored alongside their fathers in mines, mills and factories. Young girls worked with their mothers in sweatshop garment factories. Woman and child labor was widespread, abusive, and it affected poor families of every stripe. For the many ordinary Americans who remained on the farm, life was demanding and labor intensive, but they worked for themselves. If it was abusive, it was self-inflicted or imposed by the vagaries of nature. Horses and mules pulled wagons, plows and other farm implements, though tractors were beginning to appear in the countryside. Planting and harvesting were still done mostly by hand. Water was pumped from wells by hand or windmill, and neither telephone nor electric lights had yet made it to the farmer's world. Curing meat and canning vegetables were the only ways food could be preserved for any length of time.

Such were the times when this story began.

CHAPTER 2
A FLUVANNA AUGUST

Harry stood in front of the large mirror set in the oak coat and hat rack next to the entry door. He surveyed his new store-bought three-piece suit with white shirt and tie, making sure all was just so. The man he saw in the mirror was clean shaven, rangy, tanned, six feet one, with high forehead, a full head of thick, dark brown hair, and a fairly strong chin. Harry had second thoughts about the bulge in the side pocket of his jacket. He fished his smoking pipe and tobacco pouch out, laid them on the rack and smoothed the front of the jacket. He took one last look. Though feeling a little awkward dressed up as he was, he nodded his approval to the man smiling back at him. He took a quick glance at his pocket watch, returned it to his vest pocket and turned toward the door.

On the porch he encountered blue sky, bright sun and rising afternoon heat. He closed the door behind him. There was no need to lock it. As he stepped to the ground, his freshly polished shoes glinted in the dazzling sun. With one foot on the step, he effortlessly pressed his nearly 200 pounds up and into the seat of his buggy. He took the reins and released the wheel brake. "Let's go, girl. Time's a-wasting. Hup, Hup." he said as he jiggled the reins. The mare perked up her ears at the sound of Harry's voice and started walking toward the long, dirt driveway. At its end, she turned onto the county road, and Harry put her into a trot.

On arriving at Fluvanna Baptist Church, only about a country mile from home, he tied his horse to the hitching rail and paused to decide which of the two front entry doors he would use. Pastor L. H. Walton, dressed in a black suit and wearing pinch-nose glasses, opened the right door, solving Harry's dilemma.

"Hi there, Harry. You're right on time. Come on in," he said warmly.

"Hi, Reverend," said Harry. "Today's the day, I reckon. I've waited for this for a good spell, but truth be known, now that it's here I'm kind of nervous."

Reverend Walton was noticeably shorter and of a stockier build than Harry. His round face was furrowed between the brows. His lip line was thin, and when not smiling he naturally looked stern. In reality, though, he was more affable than first impressions might suggest. Motioning him to follow, the reverend continued, "Here, let me show you a place where you and I can sit and catch some breeze while we wait."

"Lead the way. I could stand a little breeze about now, being trussed up in this suit," said Harry.

As they walked, the reverend, explained, "I've done a lot of weddings, and I've yet to see a groom who wasn't nervous. Don't you worry, it's going to be just fine."

Fluvanna Baptist Church was a single-room building with two entry doors that opened into the back of the sanctuary. A large wooden cross hung behind the pulpit. The barn-style, vaulted ceiling spanned the room without support columns. The roof was clad in Buckingham slate shingles. Two aisles divided the pews into left, center and right sections.

Harry followed the pastor to a pew at the right front of the chapel next to an open window, where they sat down. "You were right, preacher, there really is a nice little breeze coming through this window."

Reverend Walton added, "It seems to come through here even when there's no wind outside. The Lord's provision, I expect." A slight smile showed his teeth.

As they continued the small talk others soon began arriving and taking seats in the pews. Some of the women talked as they waved lily pad-shaped paper fans with a funeral parlor ad printed on one side. The men folk mostly greeted each other and waited patiently. One reported that his mule had got a sharp rock stuck in the central groove of his hoof frog and was lame for three days. Another fretted over the need for rain and cooler temperatures.

At last, a certain young 25-year-old woman named Ruth arrived in a wedding dress and was quickly ushered into the church and behind a makeshift screen in the corner nearest the left entry door. There, her mother, two attendants and Ruth could stay out of sight and primp until all was perfect. After about 30 minutes that seemed to Harry like several hours, the two men heard the back door of the church open. Harry's best man, Luther Adkins, stuck his head in, spotted Harry and Reverend Walton, hurried over to them and whispered, "Everything's ready. It's time."

Harry and the reverend stood up, and the three men strode directly to a spot in the center of the room in front of the pulpit, with Reverend Walton in the lead and Harry close behind, followed by Luther Adkins. The pews fell silent. Harry was standing to the left of Reverend Walton and Luther to Harry's left. The rasping call of a cicada floated through the open windows on the occasional wisp of breeze that stirred the wilting August heat.

The smallish gathering of family and friends, about 25–30 if you count the children, were mostly seated in the first few pews of the center section, talking among themselves. A few children fidgeted uncomfortably in their Sunday best. They couldn't care less about weddings and such "girl things." Harry seemed a bit uncomfortable in his store-bought, three-piece suit. The chain of his pocket watch swagged between the vest pockets. The off-the-rack suit had a snug, tailored fit, though its sleeves and pant legs were a little too short for Harry's lanky frame. Even so he stood proudly, shoulders square, back straight.

On cue from the reverend, the organist began to pump the foot pedals of the small, upright church organ, forcing air through its pipes as her fingers played hopscotch on the keys. The congregation rose as Ruth appeared from behind the screen at the back of the church.

Harry's unconscious grin broke into a broad smile when Ruth began her slow walk down the aisle to the tempo of the wedding march. His eyes were fixed on her and hers on him, her youthful, smiling face aglow. Swells of "Here Comes the Bride" filled the chapel as she processed arm-in-arm with her father, Henry Perkins, down the left aisle and over to where the three men stood.

The white wedding dress crafted by her mother was a perfect fit for Ruth's slender, long-waisted, five-foot-six figure. The dress had no train; her bridal veil was brief. Her ensemble, though home-made, was elegant in its simplicity and entirely in keeping with the sensibilities of the Fluvanna farming community.

Ruth's medium-brown hair, when brushed out, hung halfway to her small waist. For this occasion, it was parted in the middle, framing her prominent cheekbones, then woven into two plaited strands, then swept back, covering her ears, except for the lobes, and swirled into a circle around the crown of her head. She was a lovely, statuesque, bride.

The proceedings began, and soon the pastor asked, "Who gives this woman to be wed to this man?"

Ruth's father answered, then removed his daughter's hand from his arm and gave it to Harry. Ruth's father stepped back and joined her mother in the front pew. Ruth took her place next to Harry and in front of the black-suited minister.

In that time, the average American man was only about five feet seven, and the average woman just five-feet one. Harry and Ruth both stood well above the average. Ruth's slender build, the two-inch heels of her lace-up boots and her hair bun made her appear even taller. A woman in the left section of pews leaned over and whispered to a friend, "My, oh my, don't they make a fine-looking pair?"

The other lady leaned close and whispered, "Yes indeed, they surely do, the both of them being so tall and all. I'm so happy for Ruth. It has taken her way too long to find someone. I declare, I was beginning to think she'd be a spinster."

The first lady replied, "Go on now. You ought not say such things about her. The two women looked at each other and snickered.

Reverend Walton began to speak to Harry and Ruth, and to the assembled congregation. His words, though personalized with their names, had been heard several times before by most of the folks in attendance that day. From the first note of "Here Comes the Bride . . ." to the "I now pronounce you . . ." took no more than 20 minutes. It didn't need to be any longer than that on a sweltering August day in central Virginia.

A reception followed outside in the churchyard where potluck picnics were held. Most of the women folk brought a covered dish, rolls, sweet tea, or lemonade. Someone baked a wedding cake, home made from scratch, of course. After all, it would be a few more years before ready-made cake mixes and prepackaged picnic fare were invented.

Everyone talked about how beautiful the bride was, how handsome and proud the groom. Almost certainly, some rascal brought a little extra something to give a kick to the glass of lemonade or tea held by any men who might be so inclined. The culprit was likely Luther Adkins. Though he was Ruth's age, he was a friend of both the Perkins and Morris families. Luther's easy going friendliness, round face, broad, toothy smile and cheerful manner, not to mention his charming wife, Edna, ensured his welcome at the wedding and his shenanigans at the reception.

If Ruth had ever used alcohol before this day, it would have been a rare thing, and she never smoked. Harry did imbibe on infrequent social occasions, and he smoked his pipe every day. But this day was worthy of a small sip of white lightning in their otherwise innocent beverages.

Harry and Ruth didn't have anything that could fairly be called a honeymoon as it is understood today; certainly it was nothing like a trip away for a week or two, alone together in an exotic place. More than likely, Harry lifted Ruth to the seat of his buggy and drove her to his home for their first night alone together.

CHAPTER 3
VICTORIAN PRINCIPLES

Henry W. Morris, Harry's father, had bought three adjoining parcels of land, the first in 1863, the year of Battle of Gettysburg in the Civil War, a second not long after that, and the third in 1872, during Reconstruction. He cleared some acreage for planting and another spot on which he a house. Harry was born in Cunningham District, Fluvanna County, Virginia in 1875. His parents had double cause to celebrate, as that was the year President Ulysses S. Grant ordered an end to Reconstruction in the former Confederacy. As it happened, George Armstrong Custer made his last stand at the Battle of Little Bighorn that same year, but it is doubtful that Harry's parents mourned his loss. Ruth was also born in Fluvanna County in 1886, 11 years after Harry.

In those days, a gentleman would not ask a girl's father for her hand until he was established. He had to first show that he was dependable, respectable and able to support a wife and children. Many fellows were in their mid-thirties before marrying, and Harry was one of them. He had been working his family's farm since he was a boy. He had met the standard of dependability and success. Folks around Fluvanna liked him and thought right well of him.

Girls married when they were much younger, sometimes only 15 or 16. Child-bearing years were short, and many children didn't live to see adulthood. It was important for a young wife to start having children early. That was so they would have enough children to survive childhood and to help work the farm and take care of their parents in their old age.

Ruth was 24 when Harry asked her father for permission to marry her. That was considered a little late by most folks. Maybe most of the available bachelors around Fluvanna had been a bit intimidated by her height. Maybe she was just particular in wanting a tall man. Whatever the reason, it took a little longer for the right fellow to come along for Ruth. Harry, with his height, his work ethic, physical strength and pleasant ways, proved he was the right one for her. Ruth was fertile and they were ready to start a brood of kids.

Ruth and Harry were "Victorians," as were most people in America at that time. That meant Harry was the protector, provider and leader of the family. He made all decisions . . . well, he sort of made all the decisions. Like any well-trained husband he "checked with the "Mizzez" before doing anything Ruth might think was "foolishness." So, what was so Victorian about that? Everything. Queen Victoria ruled for some 60-odd years over a British Empire that was truly global. A popular saying at that time was that, "The sun never sets on the British Empire."

The queen's beliefs and attitudes set the social standards for the entire English-speaking world, including the United States. Though long since independent, America was still culturally attached to England. Queen Victoria's beliefs about social propriety were felt in America from the mid-1800's right up until the hippy craziness of the 1960s began to push it out.

Though Harry was the final authority and disciplinarian, he reserved his punishment for the most serious childhood mischief, not that any of their kids ever deserved his discipline. Well, OK, maybe they did just a few times. Minor infractions were left to Mother and her switch. Their children learned firsthand just how handy Ruth Morris was with her switch. It could be a flyswatter, a branch from a forsythia bush or anything else that had just the right limberness to give a sharp sting to the legs or behind.

Harry was even-tempered, took seriously his duties as a husband and father, loved his family deeply and had a tender heart, though Ruth and he were both practical-minded too. Harry also had a dry sense of humor. Ruth was not what you would call a delicate flower. She could turn out just about any kind of farm work, but she also valued good grooming. Every night, after a thorough brushing, she plaited her hair into two pigtails and coiled them into a circle that she wore like a crown. She was outgoing, well composed, capable as a mother and homemaker, had an easy sense of humor and a ready smile.

Raised in a farming family, Ruth was accustomed to country living, which meant that everything had to be done by the hands of the whole family, and a woman's day began at first light. She was expected to perform all the duties of a farmer's wife, and she knew how to do what needed doing. Some of her grandchildren knew that Granny Morris could run a farm. Why, they even saw her do it.

CHAPTER 4

BLESSED DAYS AND BABES

After marrying, Harry and Ruth lived on Harry's family farm outside of Scottsville, no more than 20 or so miles from Thomas Jefferson's Monticello mountaintop home, which sits on the fringes of urban Charlottesville in neighboring Albemarle County. The Morris farm was mostly wooded, but the cleared acreage was fertile. In most years the crops were good enough to feed the family, put up a supply for winter and have some to sell to the general store in Scottsville.

America joined the First World War on April 6, 1917. Harry registered for the draft but was never called up. He was already beyond draft age, married, and their first child, Evelyn, had arrived on September 30, 1912. Their first son, Henry, was born on April 23, 1915. Edythe, their third, was born on March 17, 1917. World War I ended on November 11, 1918, at exactly 11:00 a.m., the 11th hour of the 11th day of the 11th month. It became known as Armistice Day, the day that ended "The War to End All Wars." Later it was changed to Veterans Day. For America, World War I was short and victorious. When it ended, Harry and Ruth Morris were still working the farm in Fluvanna. Christine, their fourth baby, came on October 25, 1919.

The wartime economy remained strong through that year, and Prohibition became the law of the land, sparking the era of organized crime and violence. Automatic submachine guns, notably the Thompson submachine gun, the weapon of choice for the Capone Gang, and the Browning automatic rifle or "BAR," Bonny and Clyde's favorite, became ubiquitous, and the first telephones with a dial pad were introduced.

By 1920 Harry's parents no longer lived on the farm. It was just Harry, Ruth and their kids. Like so many others at that time, they wanted a better life than the farm could provide during the postwar recession, so Harry went to Richmond to look for work. He quickly landed a job with one of the railroads that ran and still run through the city. The couple boarded up the farmhouse, packed up their kids and all their worldly possessions and headed out for a promising new life in the big city.

By spring of 1920 they were set up in Richmond. Things went well right off the bat, but a short, painful recession started in January, 1920 and lasted well into 1921. Soon after came gushing prosperity – the Roaring 20s!

According to family tradition Harry worked for the Richmond, Fredericksburg and Potomac Railroad, the RF&P. He was listed on official records as a "Fireman." On a steam engine, the fireman was responsible for starting the boiler fires and keeping them hot enough to boil the water to make steam, but not hot enough to make the engine blow up. It was hard, dirty work. The job paid enough for Harry to provide a single-family house at 1425 North 20th Street, on Church Hill, roughly a mile from St. John's Episcopal Church, where Patrick Henry famously demanded, ". . . *give me liberty or give me death!*" Luckily, their house was big enough for more kids, because their fifth child, Perkins, was delivered on February 17, 1923.

Church Hill was a pre-Revolutionary War neighborhood. In the Civil War it was the location of the largest military hospital of the Confederacy. Because of its 18th Century architecture and history it was a highly desirable place to live right up into the early twentieth century. By 1920 it had become a settlement for families migrating from the country. The Morris family fit right in.

In 1925, the banks began lending money to ordinary working people to buy cars. That's when the car industry really exploded. Everybody Harry and Ruth knew was buying them. Naturally, Harry bought one too, one of Henry Ford's ubiquitous Model-Ts. It cost around $750, plus or minus, depending on how it was equipped. We know for sure what color it was. As Henry Ford put it, "They can have their cars in any color they want, as long as it's black."

Ruth learned to drive even though she really didn't need to. Electric streetcars provided a cheap ride all over the city. A nickel or two could get Ruth to Miller & Rhodes and Thalhimers department stores on Broad Street where she could shop any day of the week except Sunday. The "Blue Law" said it was illegal for most businesses to open on Sunday. That kept businesses from forcing employees to work seven days a week. It also happened to allow families to spend more time together and go to church. America's political leaders believed that strong families and strong faith in God were essential for democracy and free enterprise to work as they should.

Beyond the conveniences of an automobile and streetcars, a family-owned grocery could be found no more than a few blocks away from home. Like all such stores at that time it delivered groceries right to the customer's door. The customer's order was carried in big wire baskets mounted on a heavy-duty bicycle. These work-bikes had heavier spokes and bigger tires and a triangular-shaped kickstand that held the bike vertical so such things as groceries and newspapers wouldn't spill out of the basket when the bike was parked.

In the summer a farmer peddled fresh vegetables and fruits harvested "early this morning" (well, maybe yesterday) from the back of his truck or mule-drawn wagon. He would ride slowly down the street dinging a small bell, and the housewives had only to walk out to the curb in front of their houses to buy just about any produce that could be found in a grocery store, and usually fresher.

In the summer, the iceman cruised through the neighborhood in his insulated, panel-body truck selling 25 or 50 pound blocks of ice for the family icebox. In the fall, the coalman delivered a load of the dusty, black rock to the shed behind the house, ready for the cast iron heating stove or fireplace when winter came.

The milkman delivered fresh whole milk or cream, chocolate or plain, in glass bottles, right to their door on whatever schedule Ruth requested. They could even deliver on Sundays if they wanted. That's because the Blue Law made an exception allowing businesses providing food, medicine, entertainment, transportation, communications and other essentials to open on Sunday.

The *Times-Dispatch*, and the *News Leader* newspapers were delivered every day except Sunday when only the *Times Dispatch* came. The Sunday paper was printed the night before and delivered to the door by dawn, so the paperboy could be finished in time for church and Sunday school. The paper was delivered by boys on those heavy duty work bikes who rode down the sidewalk tossing papers with an educated throwing arm while steering the bike and continuing to peddle without slowing down. Some of them managed with uncanny reliability to land the newspaper on the porch close to the front door.

The mail was put in the mailbox next to the front door, and a first-class stamp cost only three-cents. Imagine that. Harry and Ruth even had a telephone, one of those wooden boxes that hung on the wall, its mouthpiece sticking out like a morning glory, and a separate earpiece hanging from the end of an electric cord. It was the latest thing – no matter that four or five neighbors shared the same "party line," as it was known.

They knew whether a call was for them or a neighbor because each house on a party line had a different ring pattern. Clever huh? It was also a sure-fire way for neighbors to get to know each other and . . . uh, well . . . each other's business. The party line was the Facebook of its day. It was like a neighborhood party over the wire! That's why they called it a party line, right?

Radios were pretty expensive at that time, so Harry and Ruth might not have had one of those for the first 10 or so years after their marriage. A radio wasn't really essential because most people got their important, in-depth news from the papers, not the condensed snippets of radio news.

Most of the older houses in Richmond were being retrofitted with indoor plumbing and wiring for electric lights. Harry and Ruth certainly had electricity, and probably had either an indoor bathroom or an outhouse conveniently tucked under the back porch roof.

With all those modern conveniences, there was much more time for the kids to play. Evelyn, being the oldest, naturally put herself in charge of play time. Edythe, Christine and their playmates jumped rope and played hopscotch or jacks on the sidewalk. Edythe was unusually small and continued to be a bit thin, but she developed a full head of luxurious red hair that would make any pedigree Irish Setter jealous. It was the crown atop her very pretty face. Christine, though younger, was tall, strong and active. She took a shine to Edythe and became rather protective of her, as if she were the older sister. Henry and Perk played tag or hide and seek with their friends. Christine often joined them, but little Perkins was happy just giggling and running around getting in the way of the other kids while they played.

Ruth and Harry sometimes took their kids for a picnic at nearby Chimborazo Park. Hunting for four-leaf clovers, catching frogs and grasshoppers, playing tag or hide-and-seek, catching lightning bugs at twilight, throwing rocks off the top of Chimborazo

Hill – all were great fun for their rambunctious kids. One such outing was a walk in the park on a warmish, late autumn day. The leaves, still on the trees, were showing off their finest colors. As Harry and Ruth strolled and talked, the kids played tag, rolled in the leaves and threw pine cones at each other. It was an altogether peaceful day. Harry commented to Ruth how good their life was. They were thriving in Richmond, with good health and a bright future. All was swell.

CHAPTER 5

OUTRAGEOUS FORTUNE'S CHILD

The standard of living in America moved up rapidly during the 1920s. People were enjoying life, and the future was promising. American culture during that time seemed like a continuous party on a fast boat.

The stockbrokers had a good thing going. They would buy stocks of corporations at wholesale, mark them up and tell their investors the price was a bargain with a lot of upside profit to be realized. That part was often a good assessment, but they also lent the customers the money to buy the stock, took the stock back as collateral and charged interest rates much higher than any bank. It was called trading on margin.

The speedboat of prosperity churned up a wake of confidence that grew into waves of over confidence, spending on credit and speculating on stocks. The fast boat, with all its fun and excess, eventually crashed on the rocky shores of reality. The sinking economy took with it the hopes and dreams of most Americans.

In September and October of 1929, the stock market began to inch down. Then came Monday, October 29, "Black Monday," the day the market nosed over into a steep decline that quickly turned into a free fall. Worst of all, when the market began heading south, the brokers collected their high interest loans by selling the collateral stocks into the falling market, making it worse. It was like a lit match dropped into a bone dry wheat field on a windy day.

The experts told everybody not to worry, it was only a temporary "correction," that a "floor" would soon be reached. The market would "catch its breath," find its "legs" and run to another new high. But they were all wrong, and so were the millions of people who believed them. The stock market smashed through the expected floor like a cannonball through tissue paper and kept right on plunging. The sobering reality was that while a family's well-being was no longer subject to the whims of weather, it was now subject to even more dangerous forces beyond their control . . . man made ones.

What came next was the greatest economic hardship America has ever endured: the Great Depression. Banks and businesses soon began to fall like dominos, and so did those jobs that millions of Americans depended on. The US economy shrunk by half. Twenty-six percent of all working people were on the street. The ones who still had jobs saw their pay slashed and their savings wiped out.

Panic swept across the country, destroying everything in its path. Banks which had speculated heavily in the stock market lost millions. Families began withdrawing their bank deposits, or what was left, forcing many banks to shut their doors forever, wiping out the deposits of millions of ordinary citizens – decent, hard-working people, like Harry and Ruth Morris. Millions of Americans hunkered down. If they had any money left they stopped spending it on anything but bare necessities. Stores cut inventories, manufacturers cut production, railroads ran fewer and shorter trains, working Americans were laid off by the hundreds of thousands every month and thousands of businesses folded.

Harry and Ruth hunkered down too, prayed and waited for the storm to pass. For a time, Harry hung onto his job, but he was not exempt from the dreaded pink slip. By year's end, at age 54 he was laid off, with no assurance of when, if ever, he would be called back to work.

Public welfare in 1929 amounted to state-run work farms for men who could not or would not support their wives and children. There were also homes for the mentally or physically handicapped, who were unable to work and had no family to take care of them. There were separate reform schools for prostitutes, where they were taught morality from the Bible. All of those social services came under the "Virginia Department of Welfare." Any other assistance had to come from privately-operated charities such as the Salvation Army and Catholic Relief.

For Harry to be laid off when no other jobs were to be found was more than embarrassing, it was humiliating, even demeaning. He had not been part of the speculation in stocks. He didn't even have a stock market account. He was just a decent, hard-working husband and father with a family to support; a family who depended on his ability to earn a living, to solve their problems, to overcome any setback, to be the solid rock they could cling to in any storm.

Of course Harry and Ruth could depend on their extended family . . . if only they had not been in the same predicament. Harry sank into despair. Their kids' world was shattered, especially 10-year-old Christine and six-year-old Perkins. After weeks of searching day after day for a job and finding none, realization dawned on just how severe the Depression was, and how desperate their situation. The time had come when the Morris family could no longer put off the terrible inevitable. One night, Harry and Ruth sent the kids to bed early and went to the kitchen where they could talk without being overheard. Harry sat down in his usual seat at the head of the table, puffing on his pipe.

Ruth poured him a cup of hot chicory left over from their meager dinner. As Harry sipped his coffee substitute, Ruth quietly eased herself into the chair nearest his side. Deep lines and purple eyelids marked both of their faces, revealing their lack of restful sleep. The dream of prosperity in the city was now a nightmare for Harry and Ruth Morris, and for their children.

Harry spoke first. "I don't know what we're going to do. There just aren't any jobs to be had."

Ruth said nothing. Harry seemed lost in his thoughts for a few moments, then took another sip from his cup and curled his lips into a wry frown.

"We've got to do something soon. I do know that. If we don't we're going to run out of money," he said.

Ruth added softly, "I know. I bought eggs and powdered milk with the last of the rainy-day money from my coffee tin in the kitchen."

Harry said, "Every time I think about our children going hungry and with no home, it's like somebody stabs me right in the chest."

Ruth put a hand on his shoulder to comfort him. "Perkins can see things have changed but doesn't understand. The rest of them can tell things are in a bad way, but they'll be alright."

Harry continued, "I don't want to end up on the city farm and leave you and the kids here by yourselves. God, how I hate the thought of that!"

His face and eyes lowered, his hands wrapped around the warm cup, he thought for a moment, then added, "For that matter, I'd be surprised if the city farm has room for me."

The deepening lines in Harry's face made it plain that the uncertainty of it all, the not knowing what to do, was eating at him. Sensing that the timing was right, Ruth spoke up as cheerfully as she could muster: "Wellsir, if we have to think about you working on the city farm and leaving us here, we might as well commence to pack up and go back to Fluvanna. At least we'll all be together under one roof, and Henry, Evelyn and Edythe can help with the work. They're old enough, and a little farm work won't hurt them."

Harry lifted his chin and looked at his wife for an intense moment. "You'd do that? Go back to Fluvanna?"

"Yessir," she said, "I expect that's a sight better than you going off to the state farm. In Fluvanna we'd have no house payment, no electric, water and sewer bills, no time spent getting to and from a job. And back in Fluvanna you can't get laid off."

"Well, you've got a point there, I suppose. But are you really serious?"

"I am," Ruth answered, continuing her cheerful front. "We can make do there and keep our family together. And if we're gonna do it, I expect we ought to get started presently."

Harry continued to stare into his cup for a few seconds, not responding to her show of cheery resolve. Ruth continued looking at him in silence, her eyes betraying the worry she felt seeing the worsening strain etched into her husband's face.

They had nothing left to lose. Their faith in Washington politicians and in the ultra-rich barons of big business and Wall Street who ran the economy was shattered. The only things they knew they could count on were the good Lord, each other and that old farmhouse with its cleared patch of cropland in Fluvanna County. She could tell that Harry had already thought about going back to Fluvanna, but he could not bring himself to be the first to mention it. To his way of thinking, that would be an admission of failure.

Her proposing it took the pressure off her husband and signaled him that she was ready to not just follow him, but to stand shoulder to shoulder beside him, even in these worst of times. That day the decision was made, and the burden of having no way forward was eased. Still neither slept any more soundly that night than they had since Harry was laid off.

The next afternoon, when the kids got home from school, they were surprised to see their father at home rather than out looking for odd jobs. Ruth and Harry were going through their belongings. Christine whispered to Henry and Evelyn, "What are Mom and Daddy doing?

Henry whispered back, "They're fixing to do something, maybe go somewhere. We'd better stick close to the house today."

The word spread and all five children stayed in the yard or on the sidewalk next to the house, waiting with apprehension for their parents to tell them what was up. Soon, Ruth came to the front door and called out, "Henry, Christine, Evelyn, Perkins, Edythe. You children come on in now. Your father has something to tell you. Hurry up now. Come on." Her raised voice and her clipped words signaled that she meant *now*.

A commotion erupted as the children scrambled like a flock of chickens ahead of a hungry fox – Henry, Christine and Perkins from the front porch, Evelyn and Edythe from the kitchen. They squeezed onto the living room sofa, all except Perkins. Ruth scooped him up and sat him in her lap. Harry was already seated in his high-backed overstuffed wing chair, puffing on his pipe. The children's sudden need to sit together in a tight bunch revealed their unspoken fear and uncertainty.

Perkins whined that he wanted to get down. Ruth, sitting in a small, straight-back wooden chair beside Harry, said sharply, "Sit still and quiet down. Hush now."

Silence fell over the Morris household. All eyes were on Harry. He was looking down, his hands loosely gripping the rolled arms of his chair, his pipe clenched between his teeth, his feet flat on the floor, his knees higher than the seat of the chair. He removed his pipe, took a breath and began to speak: "You children all know I've been laid off from the railroad, and I've been looking for work for weeks now. Well, there are just no jobs to be had. We are nearly 'bout out of money. We're going to have to move." His expression was somber, his voice apologetic.

Harry and Ruth explained that they were going back to the farm where they had lived when they were first married, and where most of them were born. They pointed out that on the farm there would be plenty of work to do and they'd all have to pitch in – but farm life would be fun too. They tried to answer the kids' questions and quell their fears and protestations with words of assurance and authority.

"What will we live on, Mommy?" Perkins asked.

Ruth, avoiding the hard truth that her youngest son did not need to hear, simply answered, "Why, we'll live on love. We have plenty of that to go 'round." She slipped an arm around his shoulders, drawing him into her apron for a much-needed and rare mommy-hug.

Harry finally said, "I wish we didn't have to do any of this. Lord knows your mother and I have prayed for a job here in Richmond, but there aren't any. That's all there is to it."

He stood up and added, "I'm sorry kids, so sorry."

As he spoke those final words, he lowered his head and turned away, hiding from them the pain on his face, the redness and tears in his eyes. He walked slowly, tiredly, across the room and up the stairs, as though he were carrying a hundred pounds on his shoulders. Ruth and the children sat in silence until they heard the bedroom door close behind him.

"Alright now," said Ruth in a faux-cheery but commanding tone, "you children go wash up for dinner. Tomorrow we have to get started packing. Henry, Evelyn, Edythe, you all can pack your own things and help your father and me pack the household things. Christine, you can pack your things and help Perkins with his."

Near the end of 1929, the Morris family took everything they still owned, gave up their house, said good-bye to their friends and neighbors and moved back to the old farm that Harry and Ruth had forsaken just over a decade earlier. The way Ruth expressed it, "We just picked up what we had left, went on up to Fluvanna and commenced to living and working the farm."

The Great Depression brought about the decline of Church Hill, as more and more people like Harry and Ruth, who still owned farmland, forsook living "over the Hill" and returned to the country.

CHAPTER 6
THE DIFFERENCE A DAY MAKES

Leaving Richmond was particularly hard on the children. The house on Church Hill, the neighborhood and friends and everything they had known was ripped away. They could no longer walk to school on paved sidewalks or wait at the curb in front of their house for the produce truck, the iceman, the paperboy or grocery boy. The Morris family was not even as well off as the farmer who had once sold them vegetables off the back of his truck. Back on the farm they would at least have basic food, clothing, shelter, and, as Ruth had promised Perk, enough love to go around.

Their farmhouse in Fluvanna had no electricity, running water or refrigeration, no toilet except chamber pots and an outhouse at the woods' edge, and no paved sidewalk or driveway. The cast iron kitchen stove and a fireplace in the living room provided the only heat. It was a faded monument to a bygone era, but to Harry and Ruth, it had at least the reassuring feel of home and memories of happier days.

Immediately on arrival in Fluvanna, Harry set to working long, grueling hours from dawn to dark to get the old place in shape. Ruth, Evelyn and Henry were right there with him. Ruth put the younger ones to work too, doing what they could to help.

Improvements could be seen made day to day, and that was reassuring to them. Harry, though, drove himself. Leaving everything he had worked so long and hard to build was, to any self-respecting man's way of thinking, a disgraceful failure in his duty to provide for his family, even though the loss was caused by things completely out of his control. Harry was plagued by the fact that he was powerless to fix their plight. These thoughts of personal failure drove him. He worked tirelessly trying with everything he had in him to gain back what was lost, but he was drained. He lost weight and looked increasingly gaunt. A cough he had developed continued to dog him. Yet, Harry reached deep down in his reservoir of strength to pour himself into his work.

Before long, the house was clean, dry and tight but still in need of a makeover inside. They had acquired a mule, some chickens and a few young pigs. The shed that served as a barn was fixed up so the mule could have shelter from the wind and cold. The old pigpen was repaired too. Planting time soon rolled around and crops of hay, corn and other vegetables, and even a row of cantaloupes, were started. The kids had made friends in school, and life had fallen into a rhythm. Things were looking better, and the Morris family was feeling better about their life.

On May 5, 1930, in the afternoon after school was out, Ruth was in the kitchen just getting started on dinner. A car came bouncing down the rutted, dusty driveway. Ruth and the kids all heard it coming and went outside. They gathered in a group as it rolled to a stop in front of them. A slightly overweight, city-fide man climbed out of the car wearing a nice suit and carrying a clipboard and pencil. Henry eyed him suspiciously. The girls and Perkins looked at him studiously, somewhat fearful of the stranger.

Ruth faced him four-square in her feed sack cotton print dress and apron. "Can I help you?"

"Yes, Ma'am," said the man, in a gentlemanly, central Virginia accent, "My name is Joe Pippin. I'm from the Census Bureau office in Charlottesville, and it's census time again you know. Is the man of house here?" The children's faces changed from apprehension to curiosity.

Ruth replied in her own business-like, central Virginia accent, "I can tell you what you need to know." Ruth's tone signaled that she was in charge and could handle any business he had that needed handling.

The man continued innocently, "Oh, I'm sorry, Ma'am. I meant no offense. It's just that you look like you're busy fixing dinner right now. I can come back later."

"That's not necessary. You came all the way out here. You might as well get what you came for."

The man raised his pencil and clipboard. "Thank you, Ma'am. I'll be as brief as I can. I need the first and last name of each of you all, and your ages at your last birthday. Can you give me that?"

Ruth started with herself and proudly answered, "I'm Ruth Morris, age 42. These youngsters are my children." Pointing to each child, she proceeded: "That's Evelyn, age 17; Henry, age 15; Edythe, age 13; Christine, age 10; and the youngest one there is Perkins. He's seven."

The man asked no further questions about Ruth's marital status. He had some other innocuous questions about Ruth and her children but was soon finished. Ruth offered him a ladle of well water. He politely thanked her and declined, as he backed up to his car, got in and left. Not knowing anything about Harry, and seeing Ruth's assertiveness, he had listed her as the head of household.

CHAPTER 7
ADAPTING AND GROWING

Henry tackled the man's work that he could do. Evelyn and Edythe, being the oldest girls, worked under Ruth's supervision. Young Perkins was given such simple jobs as a kid his age could handle. For her part, Christine did all the chores she could handle. She always wanted to help when there was something useful to be done. It didn't much matter what kind of chore it was, indoor or outside.

Among the kids, they had to attend to the animals, collect the eggs, milk the cow, tend the garden, chop firewood, fetch water, help wash clothes, tend the chamber pots, clean the outhouse, clean oil lamps globes, trim their wicks and add oil, sweep and dust, beat rugs, change bed linens, help with cooking and cleaning up after, help with canning vegetables and fruit to put up for winter, and once in a while kill, dress and pluck a chicken for Sunday dinner.

Henry learned from his father how to slaughter a hog and put up some of it for curing. Other than a curing process, there was no way to preserve meat for any length of time. There were no freezers or refrigerators, though an icebox might do the job for a short time if ice had been available and if they could have afforded to buy it. Whatever part of the pig that was not to be eaten right away or put up for curing was taken to the market and bartered for other necessities.

Washday was a big undertaking. Whatever soap was available was used. Yellow "Octagon" was preferred for just about everything in the way of clothes, few as they were. Each piece was hand scrubbed on a corrugated tin washboard. When all were clean, the load was rinsed in fresh, cold water, then wrung out by hand and hung on the clothesline. Once a week, the tub served double duty for baths. Ironing involved sprinkling a little fresh water on the clean, dry clothes, then heating two flatirons on the kitchen stove, using one until it was no longer hot enough to turn the sprinkled water into steam. The second iron would then be used while the first was reheating. In this fashion there would always be a hot iron to use.

The kids walked to school except when the snow was deep. On those occasions they rode the mule. Homework was done right after they got home, followed by afternoon chores. Sometimes on Sunday the whole Morris family got dressed and went down the road to Fluvanna Baptist Church.

After their chores, the kids could stay outdoors until it was time to come in and settle down for the evening. They could go out in the woods and look for wild blueberries, wild scuppernong grapes and flowers. They especially looked for wild lady slipper orchids, Ruth's favorite wildflower. The kids could also go swimming or fishing in the creek in the warm season, play hide and seek or catch lightening bugs and put them in a Ball jar with holes in the lid to use as lanterns on warm summer nights. Occasionally one of them would find a terrapin and keep it for a few days before turning it loose again, usually with a name or initials painted or scratched on its shell.

There was also the occasional snake that had the misfortune to get caught crossing the Morris farmyard in daylight. Mostly they were blacksnakes, harmless enough, and good mousers. Sadly, the benefit of having them around was outweighed by their appetite for chicken eggs and baby chicks. When one of them was caught slithering across the yard, it usually cost him his head.

Speaking of heads, there were also copperheads, poisonous and prolific breeders. They particularly liked to nest in the stack of firewood. Green garden snakes and brown hognose snakes, both being insect eaters, slithered through the grass and vegetable garden. Occasionally a king snake would come around hunting the other kinds of snake, which were their staple diet. Evelyn, Edythe and Christine found it hard to know whether to love or hate a king snake.

Sometimes the Morris kids would catch moles, skin them, and make things out of their soft, mink-like fur. When they spotted a mole tunnel popping up across the yard they would dig their heels in front and behind the furry little fellow, then brush the layer of soil off and pick up the little guy by the nape of its neck.

Killing, dressing and skinning a mole was easy enough. It was no different than a squirrel or rabbit except for being smaller and not good to eat. The skin would be cleaned then dried and made into things such as a small purse, and several of them stitched together could make a neck warmer or hand muffler. Not that any of the kids had any money to put into a moleskin purse, mind you, but they had other treasures to put in it, things like a four-leaf clover, a colored rock they found along the creek bed, a marble or a fancy button, even an Indian arrowhead or a piece of an Indian tobacco pipe. Indian stuff sometimes turned up after a heavy rain or when the plow turned over the soil in the field.

An occasional trip to Scottsville was a family outing, and sometimes meant the kids could buy a piece or two of penny candy at the general store. When friends or family from Richmond or Charlottesville came to visit, they might bring a loaf of white bread or a dessert from the bakery. The Morris kids looked forward to having visitors who brought such things. Usually, adult visitors brought other kids to play with. The funny thing is that the folks from the city wanted Ruth's homemade biscuits and rolls while the Morris kids wanted the store-bought white bread often brought by their visitors.

Wild rabbits, squirrels, ducks and geese, maybe an occasional deer or wild turkey – anything edible that was unlucky enough to get within shotgun range – usually ended up on a platter in the middle of the dinner table. Based on what we know of Christine, it's a pretty sure bet that either Harry or Henry taught her to shoot. She was not afraid of guns and knew how to use them. Evelyn would have none of that. She simply was not cut out for that sort of thing. Edythe had no desire to learn to use a gun either.

Harry's shotgun was also used to shoot or chase away foxes, wild dogs, coyotes, turkey buzzards and other undesirable critters . . . like those snakes. They didn't shoot raccoons, or possums, or eat them either for that matter. All the Morris kids did to a possum was to startle it into playing dead, wait quietly until the ugly little fellow "came back to life" and then chase after it as it scurried away. Great fun, huh?

Dresses for the girls and shirts for the boys were rarely store bought. They were usually made from cotton feed sacks, which came in a variety of patterns and colors. Sewing was done by hand or on a manual Singer sewing machine operated with a foot pedal. Older kids' clothes were handed down. That even included shoes, coats, mittens and hats.

Edythe and Christine were less than thrilled with hand-me-downs, though that was the rule for them. With Perkins being so much younger, he would have a long wait to grow into hand-me-down clothes, so he sometimes got to wear new, homemade or store bought things.

One day, Ruth spent several hours at her foot-pedal powered Singer. When finished, she proudly held up for the whole family to see a brand new pair of pants made from a scrap of bolt cloth she had bartered at the store in Scottsville in exchange for a couple of jars of home-canned okra. Christine happened to be watching when her mother went to the screen door and called out. "Perkins!

After the third call, Perkins came scampering in, letting the screen door slam with a bang, as he hurried to where his mother sat at her sewing machine, a quizzical look on his face.

"Here, son, try on these pants," she instructed as she held them up to his waist. With the new pants on, Perkins stood up straight while Ruth inspected him.

"They're too big, Momma," he complained.

"That's alright. That's just so you have room to grow. If I made them to fit you now they'd be too little before you know it. I think they'll do. Now take them off and go on outside."

As soon as Perkins was gone Christine spoke up. Pouting a little, she whined, "How come he gets new clothes, and I have to wear hand-me downs?"

"Well," said Ruth, "You're three years younger than Edythe, so when she has grown out of her clothes, you are growing into them. But Perkins is so much younger than Henry, it would be years before Henry's would fit him. Besides, didn't I make you a dress a few months ago?"

"Yes, Ma'am, but that was made out of an old feed sack flowers on it. It's not the same thing," Christine explained.

Ruth, a little incensed by her daughter's attitude, said, "Now Christine, nobody promised you life would be fair. We have to do the best we can with what we have. I won't have you backtalking. It's ungrateful. Now go on outside and chop some kindling."

Chopping kindling was the standard chore for the younger kids' punishment that didn't quite justify the switch. Christine started to protest, "But the kindling box is full, and . . ."

"Not another word, you hear me?" Ruth interrupted. "Hush or I'll take a switch to you. Now go do what I told you."

Remembering Ruth's switch, Christine replied with resignation, "Yes, Ma'am," then turned on her heels and headed for the kitchen door, letting it slam behind her as Perkins had done. She cried through her anger and frustration as she chopped kindling. When she had a good arm load, she went back inside and stacked it on top of the nearly full kindling box. Through tears Christine went over and hugged her mother. "I'm sorry, Momma. I know you and daddy are doing the best you can. It's just that I hate having to wear hand-me-downs."

"I hate it too, little girl," Ruth said as she hugged her daughter, "but we just have to live with it presently. And besides, you can make up your mind to have a better life when you're grown. With a little common sense and hard work, you can do just about anything you set your mind to. You remember that. Now shoo, I've got work to do."

The other Morris children were a bit jealous of Perkins for the same reason as Christine, For the most part, all the kids got along well as siblings and playmates, especially Henry and Christine. They seemed to be closer to each other than to their brother and sisters, a closeness that lasted throughout their lives. Not that they didn't love the others. They certainly did, but the connection between Henry and Christine was special.

Evelyn was healthy, but she was more of a home-body, not the outdoors type, not robust like Christine. She was softer and took more interest in domestic chores. Edythe continued to get sick more often than the others and remained thin. She was a house girl like Evelyn. Chris became increasingly protective of her, almost as if Edythe were the younger of the two.

CHAPTER 8
A ROCK FALLS

Ruth climbed out of bed before dawn just like always. She didn't wake Harry or the kids. It was a little treat for them to sleep a little longer and a treat for Ruth to make breakfast by herself and have a little solitude before the day's work. As she was putting the eggs, bacon, biscuits, and milk on the table, she called out, "Evelyn, Henry, Edythe, Christine, Perkins, time to get up. You all come on now, you hear?"

She went to the bedroom door and opened it. Harry didn't stir. She let him be, closed the door and had breakfast with the children. Sun rays were beginning to stream from the eastern sky by the time they finished eating. The kids started clearing their dishes, and Ruth went back to the bedroom, this time carrying an oil lamp.

"Harry," Ruth called to him. He remained motionless. She walked over the bed, lamp in hand. She could see him plainly even in the dim lamp light. His mouth was open, his lips, ears and nose were blue. Her husband, the father of her children, their provider and protector, was dead. She gasped and stood there for a long moment saying nothing, her mind racing, then sat down on the bed beside him and wept quietly. Her five children came, stopping just inside the door. Their parents' bedroom was off limits, unless invited in. Ruth, without lifting her head, told them in her plain-spoken way, "Your father is dead."

They began to cry. Evelyn, Edythe and Christine wailed in terrible grief. Henry's eyes were wet, his face grim. Ruth stood up and wrapped her arms around her girls and Perkins, who was crying softly. Henry joined in, wrapping his arms around them all.

After a short time of grieving, Ruth pulled away. Wiping her tears, she said to Henry, "Go fetch Dr. Stinson, son. The doctor had seen Harry several times in recent weeks. He confirmed the death of Harry Morris at 11:00a.m., May 31, 1932.

Harry's death was not unexpected. You see, the reason Ruth let Mr. Pippin, the census taker, list her as head of household two years earlier was that Dr. Stinson had diagnosed Harry's cough as probably tuberculosis. He sent Harry to Blue Ridge Sanatorium in Charlottesville to be tested. At that time, TB was epidemic, killing thousands every year in Virginia alone. Harry's TB was confirmed. He was admitted but eventually returned home under Dr. Stinson's outpatient care. It had been hoped that he might fare better, but instead of extended bed rest Harry continued to work the farm and pick up other work whenever he could. His condition simply continued its slow decline, and everyone could see it. In his deeply run-down condition he lacked the strength and resistance to fight it off.

Harry was buried in the Fluvanna Baptist Church cemetery. On the way home after the funeral, the sad silence was broken by young Perkins. "Mommy, why did Daddy die?"

Ruth thought for a long moment then turned and said wistfully, "He died of a broken heart, son." That was all that needed saying. After a minute or two of silence, Ruth added, "He's in the hands of the good Lord now. We've got to look after ourselves." The silence returned and continued all the way home.

To all the Morris kids, especially the girls, their father was their solid, immovable rock that they could cling to in troubled times. But the rock fell. The Morris family pulled together and with the strength of a strong, stoic mother, they carried on. Life on the farm for Ruth and her children was at its hardest during the final stages of Harry's illness and the immediate following years, but they clung to the belief that nothing lasts forever, that there is always hope for better days ahead.

CHAPTER 9

CHANGING TIMES

On March 4, 1933, 10 months after Harry's death, Franklin D. Roosevelt was inaugurated President. His New Deal programs were soon adopted by Congress in a radical effort to create jobs and get the economy moving. Two of the first initiatives of Roosevelt's New Deal were the Works Progress Administration (WPA) and the Civilian Conservation Corps (CCC), both created in 1933. WPA developed and planned public works projects, such as building roads and bridges and adding improvements to national parks. The CCC was responsible for organizing, overseeing and paying the labor to complete the work.

Roosevelt's speeches about his New Deal revealed that he was well aware of how welfare doled out to reservation Indians without providing useful work, had robbed them of their dignity, self-respect and their proud traditions. They were reduced to permanent poverty and dependency on the same government that promised a rewarding new life.

The CCC program pumped money into an economy where cash was scarce, and that helped prime the nation's economic engine. It also helped dispel some of the cloud of gloom and hopelessness that hung like a biblical plague over the nation. That alone went a long way to restoring self-respect to millions of men who needed to work, men like 18-year-old Henry Morris. He had seen a widely circulated CCC poster that proclaimed, "A job, not a handout."

The jobs created by the program were not permanent ones, but they made a big difference during the miserable, desperate years between the economic boom before 1929 and the wartime boom that started in 1939. State law at that time had long declared that a child was a minor under parental control until age 21; but the law also allowed parents to "emancipate" a child at a younger age; that is, to let the child go and make his or her own way, to be responsible for themselves.

That term may seem odd as applied to children, but the law then was and is that parents are generally entitled to the labor of their children and at least some of the money they make. They have the right, within reason, to tell their children what work to do, how, when and where to do it. That applies to chores around the family farm or business and their home.

Parents also had the right to hire their children out and keep any wages they earned. For that reason, "emancipation" was the correct word for when a parent freed a child before age 21. Formal emancipation involved a court order releasing the parents from their responsibility for the child and the child from the duty to submit to parental authority. Often that was not done. At that time, another law in Virginia required that children of age 16 or older must support their parents if they were in need. Everyone knew that if Henry had money or labor to help his mother he would give it. It was in his nature and also in his role as eldest son to a widowed mother, law or no law.

Christine's, Evelyn's and Edythe's sense of security was shaken when the family had to leave their home in Richmond and move to the farm, a place and a lifestyle they had never really known. Their already badly shaken security was shattered when their father died. After Harry's earthly remains were buried, everyone was down and grieving. There was no fun and no joy – only essential work was getting done. They all had their tearful nights and gloomy days. Gradually, though, they began to pull together and perk up again, and things settled into a new normal for about a year.

"H-e-n-re-e!" Ruth called out from the open back door. Hearing nothing, she descended the three steps to the ground and walked out into the yard.

"H-e-n-re-e!" she called again.

"We're out here in the tool shed, Mother!" Christine called back to her.

Ruth soon appeared at the door of the shed. "Henry?"

"Yes Ma'am. Do you need me for something, Mother?"

"Yes, son, I need to talk to you. And Christine, you might as well hear it too," Ruth said.

"Yes, Ma'am," they replied, more or less in unison as they put down what was in their hands and turned to face their mother.

"You know, son, it's been tough around here, now with your father gone. You are eighteen, and I think . . ." Ruth's voice left her. She struggled to finish her sentence, but the sorrow in her heart would not allow it. Henry and Christine looked on with sympathy and breaking hearts, as they patiently waited for her to regain her composure. After a few seconds, she continued: "I don't really have any other choice, son. I need to turn you loose to go out on your own, find work to support yourself and maybe send a little money back to help us, if you can. I've already spoken to Evelyn about it just a few minutes ago."

Christine, now 13, was jolted to silence. Henry replied in his usual quiet monotone, his words clipped: "Yes Ma'am. I know. The new CCC is hiring. They'll start work presently on the Skyline Drive and Shenanandoah National Park. I hear they'll be hiring up to 10,000 men. They'll have work camps just on the other side of the Blue Ridge."

"So, you've already looked into that?" Ruth asked with surprise.

"Yes, Ma'am," replied Henry. "You know Johnny Gibson from school? He told me about it. He's going to join the CCC. He'll get three meals a day, a bed and work clothes, including boots and tools, all free. He'll get $30 a month pay. All I need to do is go with him over to Charlottesville and sign up. After that, I can leave whenever they need me and you're ready for me to go."

Ruth looked at him with pride and relief in her eyes. Christine's expression was one of surprise and pain at the prospect of her big brother and sister leaving. Ruth took in a deep breath, forced a smile, gathered herself up to her full, straight-backed height and announced as cheerfully as she could, "Alright, Henry. I expect you'd best commence to getting yourself ready." With that, she turned and walked back to the house. Henry and Christine returned to their work, but now in silence. After some time had passed, Christine turned away from her big brother and, through tears and anger, said, "I don't want you to go."

A little perplexed Henry asked, "What?"

"It makes me sad! First Daddy, now you," she answered.

He turned to her, "It'll be OK, Sis. I'll be home on weekends. Now stop your crying. That won't help." He gave her a brief pat on the back and continued, "Come on, let's finish up here."

A couple of days later, Henry rode with the Gibson boy to the CCC office, and signed up. The next day, he gathered up his few clothes, his shaving kit, toothbrush and toothpaste, his pocket-knife, pipe and tobacco pouch and a few other personal items and loaded them into a small, well-worn suitcase. When he was finished, he headed out to the front yard, suitcase in hand. Ruth and the other children, sad and missing him already, followed. He pecked a kiss on the cheeks of his mother and each of his sisters. He shook Perk's hand, tousled his hair, then turned to Ruth. "Well, Mother, I guess it's time for me to be going."

Turning to his sisters, he said, "You all have to take care of mother now. I'll be home when I can. Soon as I get paid, I'll bring some money, Mother, alright?

"That's fine, son. You go on now, you hear?"

Henry wrapped a long, sinewy arm around his mother's shoulders and held her tight, her cheek nestled to his chest. Tears once again spilled from her eyes, but she staved off the urge to break down and weep. The apron strings were cut, and both of them knew it. Henry, a little excited about his new adventure, relaxed his grip, and Ruth reluctantly pushed him away. "Go on now, son. Your friend will be along presently. You don't want to make him wait."

Eleven-year-old Perkins, who had not said a word, suddenly threw himself against Henry and hugged him tight around the waist, his tears wetting Henry's shirt. Just as suddenly, Perkins let him go and ran around to the back of the house to cry in private. With a final wave goodbye and an excited smile, Henry set off in a slow, comfortable run down the long dirt driveway. His mother and sisters watching sadly, he soon rounded the first bend and was out of sight.

Ruth turned and started toward the house. Looking over her shoulder, she said to her three girls, "Come on, we've got a lot of work to do, and we don't have Henry to help. We'll all just have to work a little harder. Christine, you're the strongest, so you'll have to help me with Henry's chores. Edythe, you and Evelyn come with me."

"Yes Ma'am," they said as they started toward the house.

"Evelyn, go find Perkins and tell him I said to chop some firewood for the kitchen stove. He was supposed to do that first thing this morning. Then pump a pail of water and carry it into the kitchen."

"Yes, Ma'am," replied Evelyn dutifully.

CHAPTER 10
MOVING ON

M en working for the CCC lived in army tents at first but soon built barracks for themselves, using army blueprints. That's because the CCC was run by the US Army. In fact, working for the CCC was a lot like being in the army, since it was the Army Corps of Engineers who provided the supervision and heavy equipment.

Henry did come home many weekends, though his visits were only overnight on Saturdays and legal holidays. His visits gradually became less often, but Henry was faithful to send money to his mother every payday and often brought some groceries, mostly things that they didn't usually have.

The CCC fulfilled Roosevelt's promise: meaningful work for meaningful pay. It was a form of welfare without stigma. Ruth, Christine, Evelyn, Edythe and Perkins settled into yet another, harder routine. The children did pick up more of the chores and, for the most part, they managed pretty well except for occasional squabbling. That was mostly between young Perkins and one of his sisters. It's hard to be a much younger brother to three sisters. Even so, they grew to be a little put out with him, because they thought he had it easier. He did, but being younger, he was not able to do everything they did.

Life on the Morris farm in Fluvanna progressed uneventfully, and the children continued to grow, both in size and ability. Ruth and Chris did the plowing with the mule and did most of the planting. Everyone helped with harvesting. Evelyn and Edythe did most of the housework. Perkins hunted, took care of killing and cleaning the game he shot, as well killing and plucking an occasional chicken for Sunday dinner, and making outside repairs to the house, shed, fences and potholes in the driveway.

Perkins soon became good at caring for the chickens and pigs. He actually seemed to like it. They would come running when they heard him coming. They associated his voice with food, and they trusted him. The three sisters got good at baking cakes and pies, canning produce and cooking meals country style. Evelyn seemed to care more about keeping the inside of the house as nice and pretty as it could be, while Christine was more interested in making clothes and trying out the jobs that she had seen her father and Henry do. As the biggest and most robust of the children still living at home, she prided herself in doing what her sisters could not.

One Friday afternoon, Henry, who was 18 at that time, arrived home for one of his overnight visits. He had already put in a hard day at work, but he brought with him groceries that he had bought in Charlottesville. With help from the girls, Ruth cooked a big dinner and everyone ate their fill. Afterward, while his sisters cleaned up the dishes, Henry went to the living room. He sat down in the big, comfortable upholstered chair near the fireplace where his dad used to sit.

Ruth and the girls were still in the kitchen, talking as they worked. Soon a faint whiff of burning pipe tobacco reached their noses. The three girls glanced at each other, then at their mother. Ruth was in another place, a faint smile on her lips, and Harry Morris came rushing back to them in warm memories and sensations of sweet-smelling tobacco, love, and happier times past.

The four slipped into the living room and stood quietly, taking in the tobacco aroma and watching the smoke curl up from the big easy chair. Ruth finally spoke. "I see you've taken up smoking, Henry."

He turned and saw them standing there. "Yes, Ma'am, I have. Do you mind if I smoke here in the living room, Mother?"

"Oh, no, son," she replied with a grin. "You go right ahead."

Just then, Perkins, now 11, came crashing in from outside. As soon as the door closed behind him, he stopped, sniffed and said, "It smells like Daddy's home."

Ruth, Edythe, Christine and Evelyn laughed. Henry smiled widely, his pipe still clenched between his teeth. Perkins wondered what was so funny. Henry continued to smoke a pipe for many years, and the aroma was always a pleasant reminder to those around him who knew and loved his father.

Since Harry and Ruth were both well above average height and of slender build, it was natural that their kids grew up even taller. By the time they were full-grown, Henry was six feet two and Perkins six feet four. Evelyn was a bit tallish for her generation, though she had grown somewhat plump. Edythe was thin, with that glorious head of red hair and hazel eyes. It seemed she was destined to be tall, but she tended to be sickly.

At five feet eight, Christine turned out to be the tallest of the girls. She had thick, shiny, chestnut hair with red highlights, hazel eyes, a narrow, concave nose, well-defined cheek bones, fair complexion, a ready smile, slender build, attractive curves and long legs. Everyone could see that she was pretty, but she seemed to be unaware of just how pretty she was. To her, pretty was useless. She put far more stock in being able to do something useful or make something creative, and to do both well.

CHAPTER 11

GAINS AND LOSSES

I n September, 1935, Christine entered the tenth grade. A few weeks later, on October 25 she turned 16. Her time to leave school and go to work had arrived. Evelyn had already gone out on her own, and was living and working in Richmond. Edythe remained at home with her mother and Perkins. Christine's leaving was long expected and was not so emotional as when Henry and Evelyn left. Christine landed a job in Charlottesville at a small restaurant on Main Street, cross from the University of Virginia Medical School.

The University Diner was made from a streamlined railroad passenger car. It was rounded on the corners and covered with brightly polished aluminum skin, a product of the art deco style of the 1930s. It sat practically next to the railroad trestle that crossed over Main Street. The restaurant looked like it belonged there, even though it was out of character with all the other buildings in the area.

Christine had no trouble finding a rooming house just a short walk from the diner. Mrs. Reardon, the lady who owned the place was about Ruth's age, had proper social manners, was widowed and was forced by the depression to take in borders. She made it clear that any males visiting Christine were welcome as long as they behaved like gentlemen and must remain in the foyer, the parlor, on the front porch or in the flower garden out back. Christine was a little embarrassed by the topic of gentlemen callers. She said she understood and did not expect any male callers, as she didn't know any. She explained to Mrs. Reardon that she got one free meal at the diner every day she worked, which was six, and would eat some meals at the Reardon house, if that was alright. Mrs. Reardon said that would be fine, but no food or hotplates were allowed to be kept in guest rooms. All was agreed and Christine settled into her room.

One of the first decisions Christine made for herself when she was on her own was to take "Chris" as her preferred name. After that, the only people she allowed to call her Christine were her immediate family and strangers who didn't know better. At the diner, Chris waited tables and baked all of the homemade pies served there. She caught the eye of many of the young men who frequented the diner. Most of them were university students. Chris, however, being an innocent country girl, did not date.

If that had not already changed, it certainly began to change months later when Emmett Payne walked into the diner. He was about five feet nine, muscular, with a strong jaw, thin, light brown hair, a high forehead and pale blue eyes. He noticed her right away. She noticed him too, but ignored him until he couldn't stand it any longer.

Emmett described her as "drop dead gaw-jus," and a "knock-out," which explains why he became a daily customer. Whenever he came, he was careful to sit where she would wait on him. He would often buy a slice of whatever pie she had made that day, his favorite being apple. He always left a tip and showed her his best manners. This attractive, muscular fellow was not a student at the university. He was a local who worked as a plumber and steamfitter on a contract job at the university's medical school.

His attentions and good manners were more than Chris was used to from most of the rough-and-tumble construction trades-men and university students. Some of them were ill mannered, or leered at her. Her boss tried to protect her from those, but he couldn't be standing over her all the time. She soon learned how to put those customers in their place with a few ready comebacks that left them feeling outsmarted and embarrassed. Emmett though was not at all like them. When she decided she had ignored him long enough, Chris allowed Emmett to talk to her.

He soon invited her out and she accepted, though he was nine years her senior. Their dates often were nothing more than a stroll around the University grounds, an occasional movie, or a visit to Emmett's parents house. When Emmett could afford gas, their fa-vorite place to go was to drive up on the recently opened Skyline Drive along the top of Afton Mountain. They sometimes went for a picnic on one of the scenic overlooks there.

Around the time Christine left school and took her job at University Diner, Edythe became sick. When she did not get bet-ter in a couple of weeks under Ruth's home remedies, Dr. Stinson was asked to make a house call to see her. Like her father, she had come down with tuberculosis. Her disease consumed her rapidly. When she was near death, all the Morris children joined Ruth at home in a death vigil. Edythe passed away on May 31, 1936. She had just turned 19 in March.

On that same day the radio news reported that the German government had announced it was building a new fleet of naval vessels. That was a violation of the Versailles Treaty that ended World Wear I, but it was seen as a program to fight the depression that ravaged Germany as well as the rest of the industrial world. All of that was lost on the Morris family, who had more important and personal concerns to deal with. When it came time to dress Edythe's hair for the funeral, Chris insisted that she do it, and she did, tenderly, lovingly. Like her father, Edythe was buried in the church cemetery at Fluvanna Baptist. After the funeral, Chris returned to her job at the diner.

Late in the following July, Emmett came to the diner, one of his many visits there for coffee, apple pie and to see Chris. Between bites of pie Emmett suggested that they go out the next Saturday, which was a rare weekend day off. Chris agreed, and when the time came he picked her up in the used car he had bought. It was still daylight and they drove up Route 250 to the top Afton Mountain, then along Blue Ridge Parkway to a scenic overlook where they could watch the sun go down.

They strolled to a more-or less flat rock jutting out over a steep drop down the mountain side where they sat down and just talked and looked out over the Shenandoah Valley toward the Appalachian ridge on the other side. They sipped a pair of Coca Colas and munched on some Lance crackers while they talked. After a while they grew quiet and just stared at the view. Emmett leaned over and gave Chris a peck on the cheek. She turned her head toward him and they kissed.

He said quietly, "You know how crazy I am about you, don't you?"

"Yes, and I kind of like you too, a little." she said teasingly."

He grabbed her around the waist and pulled her close. "Come on," he said playfully, "I know you love me as much as I love you."

Chris laughed, elbowed him in the ribs, laughed again, then laid her head over against his and said more seriously, "Yes. I do."

"In that case," he said, "I have something for you." He went to the car for a moment and returned. He resumed his position next to her and held up a small cardboard box. Chris looked at the box, surprised, a little uncertain but eager. He handed it to her and waited with a smile. She carefully opened the box to see a beautiful, brilliant round-cut, citrine stone in a gold solitaire setting. It's deep color resonated with the orange rays of the setting sun. Chris was thrilled to tears as she smiled and looked lovingly at Emmett.

"Oh Emmett, it's beautiful!" she exclaimed, then leaned over and kissed him all over his beaming face.

Amid her shower of kisses Emmet said, "I guess this means your answer is yes?"

Chris laid her palms on each side of his face, gazed into his eyes and said, "Yes, yes!

Their lips met again for a warm, tender kiss.

Chris thought wistfully for a moment then said, "I wish we could get married now."

Emmett replied, "Me too, and we can if your mother signs the papers."

"But she won't. She didn't marry my father 'til she was in her twenties. She'll say I'm too young, and we haven't known each other long enough." Chris explained.

Emmett said, "You'll turn 17 in two months. Another year after that and we won't need her consent."

Chris said, "But that seems like such a long time."

"Well, there is one thing we can do." Emmett said.

"What?"

"Well, anybody that looked at you would think you're 20 or 21." Emmett answered." We could apply for a license and tell them you're 21. They wouldn't doubt it for a minute."

Chris answered skeptically, "Oh, I don't know. It wouldn't be right"

Emmett persisted, "The way we feel is right, isn't it? And what if it doesn't work? They won't give us the license and we just leave."

Chris thought about it for a few days and talked with her mother about the idea of marrying. Chris's guess about Ruth's attitude was correct. In the end, she and Emmett took their mandatory blood tests to check for genetic disorders and communicable diseases. Soon, they had the test results and were issued a marriage license. On the application for the license, Emmett wrote that Chris was 21, and she kept quiet. They were married on August 8, 1936, in Palmyra, Virginia, by Methodist pastor, Reverend Ledford C. Vaughan. It was a short, simple ceremony witnessed by a couple of friends. Their honeymoon was a three-day weekend in Richmond. On their return to Charlottesville, they stopped at the farm and told Chris's mother what they had done. She was terribly disappointed, but she couldn't complain about Emmett being too old for her daughter, considering the age difference between Ruth and Harry. She remained stoic, and in the end wished them well.

Before long, the newly weds moved permanently to Richmond in search of a better life, just as Ruth and Harry had done almost a generation earlier. Once back in Richmond, Chris became a homemaker. Emmett had a job with Virginia Electric and Power Company, which later changed its name to Dominion Power. "VEPCO", as the company came to be known, owned and operated all electric streetcars in Richmond, as well as the electric power lines and generators. Most of the generators were coal-fired steam boilers, which created a lot of work for steamfitters, plumbers and mechanics – just the ticket for Emmett.

He and Chris rented a row house on Robinson Street and settled right in. The electric streetcars, as they once did for Ruth, could get Chris anywhere she wanted to go. Emmett still had the used car he had when he met Chris, but he walked the few hundred feet to where he worked at the power company "car barns," as they were commonly known. That was a group of buildings where electric streetcars were garaged and repaired. The name was a holdover from when streetcars were horse drawn. Emmett's working so close to home allowed Chris to use their car as she wanted when Emmett was at work.

Things for Chris were just as she remembered from her childhood on Church Hill. The life her family had known and lost was hers again. Like Ruth before her, Chris got down to starting a family soon after the vows were exchanged. Ruth and Perkins also found jobs in Richmond. They boarded up the old farmhouse once again and were back in Richmond, though not on Church Hill.

Chris and Emmett's firstborn, Gene L. Payne, arrived on December 22, 1937, delivered at home by Dr. Hulcher, who was ably assisted by Ruth herself. According to Chris, the only reason for birthing her first child at home was that she felt more comfortable there, and there was no hospital bill. The way Chris figured it, her mother had birthed five children, all at home. Ruth had been there and done that. Chris had more confidence in her mom than in the doctor.

Baby Gene's middle initial "L" was for Lamar. As Chris told it, she'd really wanted her firstborn to be a girl and intended to call her Jean Lamarr, with the middle name taken from movie actress Hedy Lamarr. When her baby turned out to be a boy, Chris changed the spelling to Gene Lamar and went with it. Emmett, giddy over being a dad and being open to unorthodoxy, was happy with the name. Twenty months after Gene was born, Chris and Emmett's second child, Charles Edward Payne, arrived on August 8, 1939, their third wedding anniversary.

Baby "Charlie" was named for Emmett's dad, Charles Byron Payne, while "Edward" was for Chris' dad. Some might say Gene and Charlie were "Irish Twins," being born only 20 months apart, but they proved to be different in many ways. At the time of Charlie's birth in Richmond's Grace Hospital, Chris and Emmett still lived on Robinson Street. Eventually they moved to a rented, single-family house on Idlewood Avenue, a little east of Byrd Park but still within easy walking distance to the VEPCO car barns.

Chris and Emmett had a telephone in their new place. It was still a party line, though the phone itself was made of an advanced, man-made material called "bakelite." The phone was a fraction the size of the old one and sat on a table instead of hanging on a wall. The new phone looked a lot like a candlestick with a dial pad on the base and a microphone shaped like a daffodil blossom. They quickly became known as candlestick phones.

With the Depression now quickly melting away and the hounds of war baying in far-away Europe, prosperity began to return to America. In 1939, when Perkins turned 16, he followed in Henry's footsteps and joined the CCC. Henry married a girl named Elizabeth, and soon they had children too.

All four of Harry and Ruth's living children made their way back to Richmond. Henry, Chris and Evelyn lived independently but not all that far from each other. Perkins lived with Ruth for awhile after leaving the CCC. Family contact was regular, especially between Henry, Chris and Ruth. Life seemed to be getting better in every way.

By 1940, no one was living on the farm in Fluvanna. Harry's father, Henry W. Morris was the sole owner of the property, and he had died. Ownership of the property passed to his descendants. Harry's share passed to Ruth and her children. Shares were also inherited by Harry's siblings. Vincent Morris, Harry's brother, contacted Ruth about dividing up the property. That turned out to be impractical and they were left with no choice but to sell the property. The problem was that not everybody wanted to sell it.

A law suit was filed by Evelyn, Henry, Chris and Perkins against Vincent Morris and his siblings, asking the court to order the property sold and the proceeds divided up among the heirs. It was not done out of anger. Rather, it was the only way it could get sold. The suit made its way through the Circuit Court of Fluvanna County. Eventually it was ordered that the property be auctioned off to the highest bidder.

On December 4, 1940, the auction was held on the court house steps in Palmyra. The Special Commissioner, W.N. Hannah, went through the preliminaries of reading the court order and calling forward all interested parties. It turned out that the only people who stepped up were the heirs and one stranger. The bidding began.

"Alright, who will be the first to bid on this property? It is 198 acres, more or less, of fine tillable fields, with a two story house and valuable woodland," said the Commissioner as he looked at the faces of each person present. No one spoke.

"Come on now, who'll make the first offer?" he repeated. Still no bid was heard. He looked again at each person and asked, "How about you?" They all looked around at each other only to see blank looks or a slight side-to-side movement of the head.

Finally, Vincent spoke up. "I guess everybody who might want it is like us. We're all still hurting from the Depression, and the lives we want don't involve farming."

Ruth answered, "Well we've come this far. It would be a shame for it not to get sold."

General murmuring rippled among the group. Commissioner Hanna finally called it to a head. "Well, what do you all want to do?"

A long, pregnant silence fell. Then, Ruth spoke up. "Wellsir, something told me this might happen. I have $600. I'll put that up. It's a pitiful price to pay for the place, but that's all I can afford."

No one dreamed that Ruth Morris had any money that she was willing to bid for the place. There were no other offers, and the property was knocked down to Ruth P. Morris. On February 7, 1041, she paid the money and received the deed to the entire 198 acres and house. Was it just happenstance, or did she plan it? We'll never know, but we do know that she sold it in 1954, for $2,400, after some timber had been harvested and sold. Not bad for a country girl.

Those who lived through the Great Depression grew lean, tough and resilient. They learned the hard way that prosperity is not guaranteed, that neither the government nor big business nor

Wall Street could be trusted to protect the little guy or to fix all the problems that ordinary folks face. From the hardships of the Depression, they developed a quiet confidence that if they stuck together, worked hard and used their brain they could overcome any catastrophe, any setback, any threat to their freedom and prosperity.

The war in Europe had been grinding on for two and a half years while America remained neutral. President Franklin Roosevelt, with Congressional support, entered the Lend-Lease program with Britain. The US sent ships, tanks, airplanes and other military equipment and supplies, as well as food and medicines, to Britain on the promise that they would pay for all of it at the end of the war if they won it. Similar arrangements were made with Russia. America had already begun to build up its own defenses, and the rapid increases in jobs brought an end to the last vestiges of the depression.

Then, on December 7, 1941, America was swept into the vortex of World War II by the Imperial Japanese Navy's attacked on Pearl Harbor. The US declared war on Japan, the very next day, and Germany, Japan's ally, declared war on the US the day following that. Despite that global nightmare, things in Chris's family seemed to only get better. Money was flowing and people once again felt flush.

Emmett, who was 31 when Pearl Harbor was bombed, was exempt from the military draft because his job was considered a critical occupation. After all, factories need electricity to turn out war supplies, and factory employees had to get to work on the electric streetcars and busses. Henry was also exempt from the draft for the same reasons as Emmett. Perkins, now called "Perk," turned 18 on February 17, 1941. He registered for the draft and was eventually called up and inducted into the army after Pearl Harbor.

Before shipping out, he came home on leave once or twice, bringing along a buddy named Scotty. The two young soldiers were both happy-go-lucky guys, seemingly unconcerned about the war that awaited them. But that's just it. They both knew they might die, and they accepted it. That led them and a lot of young soldiers just like them to grab hold of every minute of time and squeeze it for all the life they could wring out of it. Perk soon shipped out to Europe and was not seen for a long while.

Because he was such a tall, strapping fellow, he was assigned to the military police. Those were the guys who went to the front lines with the infantry and tanks to round up all the captured Germans, disarm them and take them to POW camps. Of course, the MPs also patrolled the streets of liberated or captured cities and towns, and responded to any calls concerning American GIs in bar fights or drunk on the street. Though not infantry, artillery or tank troops, the military police were often at or near the front lines and faced a variety of dangers. Among them were Germans behind American lines posing as American soldiers, enemy air raids and artillery fire. It is a safe bet that Ruth, Henry, Chris and Evelyn, and a certain young lady named Jesse prayed regularly for Perk's safe return, and with good cause.

During the war, when a sad mood welled up inside her, Chris would sit at the piano and play "Danny Boy." Her phrasing of the notes was melancholy. It was her way of expressing her anguish and fears not only for Perk, but for all those millions of American boy-men whose lives were in harm's way.

CHAPTER 12

I CLIME COUH

One warm day in late spring of 1942, Chris was in her kitchen. On the radio, the news reported that what was left of the US Navy after Pearl Harbor was holding off the Japanese Imperial Fleet in the Battle of the Coral Sea. At stake was whether the Japanese would gobble up Australia and New Zealand or be stopped. Chris listened intently, hoping the reporter would say the battle was won.

Little Charlie was out in the back yard busy making mud pies and "cooking" them on the metal wing of the pedal plane that he shared with Gene. After his pies were cooked dry in the warm sunshine, Charlie took a bite of one. It was gritty, and even the worm inside it didn't help the taste. He spit it out and looked for something else to do.

About that time he heard the boy who lived next door come outside. He was Charlie's age. Although they had talked to each other through the high board fence that separated their yards, he and Charlie had never seen each other, much less played together. Chris and Emmett didn't get to socialize with the people who lived next door. Both the man and his wife worked every day and left their little boy with a sitter.

One day Charlie just up and decided it was time for him to see the boy next door and maybe play with him. Emmett had bought an old car to fix up for Chris. It was parked up close beside the backyard fence. Charlie climbed up on the rear bumper, then on the taillight that stuck out on a spindle from the fender, then to the top of the trunk and onto the roof. In less than a minute, Charlie was on top of the world looking down into the yard next door where the little boy was playing.

The boy was busy trying to pick up a big rubber ball, but every time he ran up and reached for it, his foot kicked it away. After watching him for a little awhile, Charlie spoke to the boy. "Wuh ya doin?"

The little guy next door knew Charlie's voice but not his name. He stopped and looked toward the fence, but he didn't look up.

"Playin'," he replied, looking left and right but not seeing Charlie.

Charlie said, "I see ya,"

"Do not," said the boy, looking side to side at the fence, his forehead wrinkled.

"Uh huh, you chas'n ball," said Charlie.

The boy again looked all around, but not up.

"Wheh you?" He asked.

"Up heah," said Charlie, as he put his hands on top of the fence and leaned on his arms.

The boy looked up and saw him. Amazed and surprised, he asked, "Hah ya get up dare?"

"I clime couh," said Charlie, as if there was nothing to it. "Wha' yo name?"

"Andy," the boy replied. "Wha' yo name?"

"Chaulie"

"Kin ya come down an' play?" asked Andy.

"OK," said Charlie eagerly. Holding onto the fence, he threw one leg over and rested his foot on the board nailed long-ways to the other side. Before he could swing his other leg over, a loud shriek came from the kitchen window.

"No, Charlie! Get down from there!" Chris shouted, fear giving bark to her voice.

Charlie heard her and the sound of things being dropped, running footsteps, kitchen table sliding across the floor and a chair falling over, as Chris headed for the door. Her tone and all the commotion scared little Charlie. He got his lag back over the fence and scurried as fast as he dared toward the place where he climbed up. Chris burst through the screen door, making it bang against the wood siding. Charlie was at the edge of the car's roof when Chris shouted again, "Stop Charlie! I'm coming!"

As the words left her lips, the smooth, leather soles of Charlie's toddler shoes slipped on the rounded slope at the edge of the car's roof, and he fell to the ground with a thump and the sound of breaking glass. In a blink, Chris leaped from the porch and was at his side, on her knees, her heart pounding against her chest. Charlie's crumpled body lay on the ground, blood running onto the dirt. He was conscious but screaming. Shattered pieces of a glass milk bottle lay next to him. Bright red blood covered Charlie's left eye and the side of his face.

Chris lifted him gently into her arms, cradling his head in her hand. There, on the ground where his head had lain was a bloody glass shard with a sharp tapered point sticking up. Chris cried out, "Oh God, please, no!,"

She jumped to her feet, her little boy clutched in her frantic embrace, and dashed to the house. She sat him in his highchair and sopped the blood with a tea towel, which was soon red. The blood continued to flow freely. She ran to the bathroom and retrieved a bath towel, ran back to the kitchen and wrapped the towel around his bloody head. Chris then called Ruth, who lived only a block and a half away on Grayland Avenue. Charlie could not see anything with his left eye but bright red. The towel covering his head was soon blood-soaked and sagging down over both eyes, causing him to see only blackness and red. That terrified poor Charlie all the more.

Ruth Morris soon arrived. Fearful but under control, she unwound the bloody towel and immediately saw blood still running from Charlie's head. Using a dry corner of the towel to wipe the fresh blood from Charlie's face, she saw the deep, jagged cut in his temple directly beside his eye. Ruth applied a fresh towel and held it over the left eye and left side of Charlie's head, being careful not to press directly into the gash. His good right eye was now uncovered, so he could at least see with that one. His screams and the bleeding both began to subside as Ruth pressed the towel against his head.

Charlie looked around and saw Gene standing close by, looking up at him. Gene's eyes were wide, his mouth hanging open, and fear was on his face. Charlie started crying all over again. Chris shooed Gene to the living room as Granny Morris calmed his brother.

"It's alright, Charlie," said Ruth, "you'll be just fine, presently. Mommy and Granny will take care of you. Hush now. Don't worry. The doctor will have you good as new. You'll see."

In the state of urgency, Ruth did not intend or grasp her play on words. While Ruth comforted Charlie, Chris went out and got the car started. Emmett ran all the way from the car barns, arriving just as Ruth, with Charlie in her arms, reached the open door of the car. The look of fear on Emmett's face frightened Charlie all over again. Chris slid over and took him in her arms, while Emmett got behind the wheel. Ruth stayed behind to look after Gene. She shut the car door just as it sped off toward Grace Hospital's Emergency Room.

At the hospital they learned that Ruth had called ahead and the duty staff was waiting. An orderly opened the door for Chris and the baby, took her by the arm and the two of them rushed into the hospital while Emmett found a place to park. Soon he joined Chris in the emergency room. They waited, prayed, Emmett paced and Chris was lost in frightening thoughts of Charlie being blind in one eye.

After what seemed like a hour or more, a doctor walked out wearing a blood spattered white smock with surgical mask dangling around his neck, a sweaty white cap covering his hair. He called out, "Mrs. Payne? Mr. Payne?"

Chris stood up and Emmett quickly came to her side. Both bearing the deep furrows of fear and worry, they were frozen in place. The doctor quickly came over to them, "Are you the parents of the child with the cut near his eye?" he asked.

"Yes," answered Chris anxiously.

"Your son is going to be just fine," he said. Breaking into a slight smile he continued, "The glass did not puncture the eye or the temporal bone. Your son was very lucky. It was close, but he's fine. The cut was irrigated with saline to remove any pieces of glass, doused with iodine and repaired with five stitches. He's ready to go home."

In a week's time, Charlie was good as new and rambunctious as ever. After an experience like that one might think a child that age would have lost his desire for climbing fences. But that would not be Charlie. A few months later, he again attempted to reach Andy. This time it was by climbing the locked gate in the picket fence on the side of the house.

He managed to get himself straddling the pickets before Civil Defense air raid sirens started wailing. Charlie got scared and started to cry. Suddenly, along came a monster with two great big eyes and a trunk like an elephant that ran down from its face to a box tied around the monster's chest. It rushed at him and grabbed him up from the fence. Charlie screamed, fearing the monster was going to eat him. Fortunately, Chris came out the front door, rushed over and rescued little Charlie from the monster's clutches.

Holding him in her arms, she said, "Look, Charlie. Look. It's OK. It's only an air raid warden. And he's wearing a gas mask. See?"

Charlie turned just in time to see the monster rip its face off. Beneath it was a human face, smiling and saying nice things to him. Still, Charlie didn't like that man. He might turn back into the monster and eat him. Gene heard the commotion and came out, only to see his little brother screaming again. He came over and tried to help Chris reassure his younger brother. Seeing that Gene was not afraid of the monster-man, Charlie accepted that he was safe.

Sometime later, Charlie again climbed the car in the backyard. This time all his weight was on Andy's side when his foot slipped and a rusty nail in the fence took a plug out of his leg just above the knee. He got himself down and ran to Chris as fast as he could, leaving a chunk of flesh hanging on the rusty nail. Chris, having been through this before, was cool. She just took him inside, doused the wound with witch hazel and tied a tea towel around the leg. Gene barely noticed and stayed home with Ruth, while Chris took Charlie to the doctor, who stitched him up, gave him tetanus and penicillin shots, and sent them home.

Even Charlie seemed to take that one in stride. Another five or six stitches, a week's time, and he was good to go. That third climbing incident did not, however, cure him from wanting to play with Andy, nor from climbing nor getting hurt. Chris promised him that she would talk to Andy's mother and see if she would get the sitter to let Andy and Charlie play. For unknown reasons Charlie never got to play with the boy next door.

When he was a little older, Charlie made a habit of climbing the tallest trees he could get up into, just for the thrill of being up high and seeing far and wide. He fell out of two of them but he never lost his joy of climbing the heights. Gene was never interested in that particular form of play. Charlie continued to get cut, punctured, contused and bruised. Chris got to where she would just stop the bleeding, put a patch on his latest injury, chuck him in the car and cart him off to the doctor or the emergency room. Before long she was unflappable and pretty well trained in emergency medical care.

Gene had better sense than his younger sibling. He was content to leave the tall trees and board fences alone. Far more civilized than Charlie, he played games, listened to the radio, colored in his coloring book, drew pictures and such. Charlie, on the other hand was in perpetual motion when he was awake. He didn't want to miss a thing, so he was outside doing something, anything, investigating everything he saw or heard and often getting in the middle of whatever he encountered.

Chris remained ever busy, ever curious and intrigued by Emmett's projects, just as she had been with big brother Henry back on the farm. She continued to make baby clothes on her sewing machine, bake and cook, read mystery novels, talk with other housewife friends and tinker with Emmett's projects, including mechanical, electrical and plumbing ones.

CHAPTER 13

TOGETHERNESS

O ne day, Chris put Charlie in the back seat of the family car
and drove the eight or nine blocks to where Emmett worked
to take him his lunch. Gene was either in nursery school or was
left at home with his Granny Morris. When Chris pulled into the
parking lot at the car barns, Emmett came out to meet them. Chris
rolled down the window and handed him his brown paper lunch
bag. He and Chris talked for a minute, then he kissed her, said a
few words to Charlie and waved goodbye.

As Chris began to pull away, Charlie stood up in the back seat
and watched through the rear window as his dad, waving and smiling, shrank into the distance. Seeing their mommy and daddy
showing affection for each other always made Gene and Charlie
get all giddy inside. It's a mystery how that is.

Around the same time, Emmett built a toy airplane out of wood
from orange crates. He covered the frame with cloth and painted
it. The airplane had a wood plank seat and was big enough for either of the boys. The toy airplane even had a working control stick
that moved ailerons and elevators. When it was finished, Emmett
put his boys in it, one at a time, and "flew" them around the yard
over his head. The boys cried out, "Eee-yauw, eee-yauw, eee-yauw,"

which is what they imagined their airplane would sound like. The three boys – one big two small – laughed and giggled, while Chris watched and wore a smile.

One Saturday morning, Gene and Charlie woke up while Chris and Emmett were still asleep. The boys went to their mom and dad's bed. Gene could reach his daddy, but Charlie had to climb up on the bed to get to his mommy. The two boys patted Chris and Emmett on the shoulder and whispered in their ear, "Wake up, Mommy. Wake up, Daddy, wake up."

After two tries at patting their shoulders to no avail, the boys resorted to patting their parents' cheeks as they whispered. Chris and Emmett finally rolled over and looked at the boys through bleary eyes. Chris said, "Not yet boys, Mommy and Daddy are still sleepy. You boys go play quietly in the living room for a little while, OK?"

Gene and Charlie did as they were told . . . for a little while. But to their tummies it seemed like a long time. Soon, the boys couldn't wait any longer. You know those peg boards that toddlers play with, the ones with the little round pegs in holes and a wood mallet to hammer them with? Yeah, Gene and Charlie had one of those. They took their pegboard and mallet to mommy and daddy's room, sat on the floor next to the bed and took turns banging the pegs with the mallet. Hammer them through, turn the board over, and hammer the other way. It was loud. It was Gene's idea, and it worked.

Chris and Emmett dragged themselves out of bed and got busy sharing the tasks of "pottying," washing and dressing the boys and making breakfast. Neither Emmett nor Chris really understood that those two tykes knew exactly what they were doing, planned the ruse and pulled it off perfectly.

One day, when Gene was about four and a half years old and Charlie about three, Chris and Emmett took them down to the James River to watch a ship unload scrap metal from the war. A sizable crowd was also there to watch. Chris had Gene straddling her hip. From there, he could see just fine. Though Emmett was holding Charlie the same way, Charlie wanted to see over all the people's heads. He wanted to see a Nazi swastika. After begging his daddy, Emmett hoisted him up onto his shoulders. Charlie, now up high, could see everything, including, for the first time, the bald spot growing on top of his father's head.

That day, Gene and Charlie saw a giant, iron dinosaur with a huge mouth and big iron teeth biting into the Nazi war machines, ripping them apart and piling the pieces on top of a mountain of Nazi scrap metal. It wasn't long before the iron dinosaur, with a mighty roar, raised its head out of the belly of the ship and swung around with a chunk of Nazi fighter plane dangling from its toothy maw. The dinosaur opened its jaws and let the dead airplane fall to the top of the heap. There on the plane's tail section sticking up in the air was a swastika. Chris and Emmett both excitedly pointed it out: "Oh, look! Look boys. See the swastika?" Gene and Charlie had already spotted it. Seeing that big American iron dinosaur chewing up the Nazi war machines was great fun for Gene and Charlie, because they got to see that America was beating the "mean ole' Nazis."

Those few short years were a time when their boys ruled and Chris and Emmett were devoted to them and to each other. During these good times, Chris hand-made most of the clothes her boys wore. She told them that when they were older and saw her making children's clothes for other people. The things she made looked just like they had come from a department store. Ruth had taught her well.

Chris made dresses, skirts and blouses for herself and a few of her girlfriends, as well as pleated, lined window curtains, all looking like they were store-bought. She liked to keep busy and was always working on something in addition to cooking, cleaning, doing the wash and taking care of her family.

Once in a while Chris and Emmett attended the Baptist church, taking a short walk to the end of the block, around the corner, cross the street and they were there. On one such occasion they were seated on the end of a pew in the crowded sanctuary. Gene was next to his dad and Charlie next to Chris as the preacher, dressed in all black, delivered his sermon.

Speaking in a light, conversational tone, he droned on. As he neared his main point, he began to get wound up, talking faster and louder. When he came to the grand, climactic point of his sermon, he started shouting and pounding the pulpit with his fist. His delivery, though in vogue at the time, scared poor Charlie so badly that he began to cry. Chris picked him up and cuddled him, shushing him softly, to no avail.

The preacher raised his voice more and carried on his haranguing, and Charlie raised his voice and carried on his wailing. Soon it was clear that one of them would have to leave. Chris picked Charlie up and slipped out. Emmett and Gene followed. Apparently none of the family enjoyed that sermon any more than Charlie. It seems that Chris and Emmett stopped going to church soon after that.

CHAPTER 14

SMOLDERING EMBERS

As the tempo of war hastened, the economy grew ever stronger, and manpower for civilian jobs was growing scarce. That's when Chris began to think about going back to work. There were many traditionally men's jobs available that were now being filled by women. Still, Chris enjoyed being a stay-at-home-mom, and she dreamed of yet having a little girl. She adored babies! It didn't matter whose it was, she always gushed and wanted to hold and cuddle the precious little ones. That was one of her most endearing and enduring traits, and she was completely unabashed about it.

Despite all of her dreams and aspirations, there were other factors that set her to thinking. One of those was that her mom, Ruth, had landed a good job baking cakes at the Bond Bread Company plant and had told Chris they were hiring women for a variety of job openings. The big thing gnawing at Chris and that kept her thinking about returning to work was right at home. It was Emmett. The good days were increasingly interrupted by bad nights.

Emmett had grown more and more controlling and possessive. His jealousy went along with increased drinking and a violent temper. Chris, for her part, could argue the paint off a wall, and she was stubborn and independent. She was no longer giving Emmett positive strokes – words of appreciation, encouragement and approval, a spontaneous and sincere hug, or a simple, "I love you." It was a chicken-and-egg dilemma.

Emmett's drinking to excess and temper outbursts were fueled by Chris's good looks, cheerfulness and outgoing personality. His faults were rooted in his own insecurities and the fact that he was nine years older than Chris. Any slight friendliness by Chris toward another man was seen by Emmett as flirting. His mind was tortured by imagined infidelity. That may very well have been reinforced by the lack of those positive strokes from her. Yet he seemed unable to see the connection between her diminished affection and his own failings.

Through Ruth, Chris took a job in 1942, driving a route delivery truck for the Bond Bread Company. She was one of four young women hired to take over jobs vacated by men going into the service. *The Richmond Times Dispatch* even did a story with a photo about her and several other young Bond Bread girls. Chris enjoyed being part of a team of women who contributed to the war effort by holding down a man's job. She liked the job, the camaraderie, the pay and the sense of pride. Emmett, however, driven by jealousy and suspicion, was actually seen on at least one occasion skulking around the Bond Bread plant, spying on his wife. To say that humiliated and infuriated Chris would be an understatement.

Emmett, for his part, would sometimes just disappear after work, go bar hopping then show up at home hours late and drunk. Maybe he did that in retaliation for the imagined indiscretions on her part. That will never be known. Despite all of that and more, he had his good qualities too. He was generous, compassionate, hard working, accepted his responsibility as provider, was honest, paid his bills, readily showed affection and laughed freely and often – when he was sober.

Chris shared these traits with him, and to boot, she grew to be self-confident, assertive and could be relentlessly stubborn when she was convinced she was right about something. If you think it might be easier to pet a hungry alligator than squeeze her into the mold of a passive housewife, you'd be right. To make matters worse, she was much smarter than Emmett in God-given brain power. In fairness to him, though, he was imaginative, handy at making things and had a knack for spinning imaginary tales, usually funny ones.

Even so, the smoldering embers of discord between the two were slowly burning away the timbers of trust, peace and unity that every marriage needs in order to endure. In reality, Chris just wasn't especially demonstrative toward Emmett, and, as it turned out, not much toward their two sons, once they were beyond kindergarten. Her love and devotion to her boys could be seen in other ways, but not by a mother's tender words, hugs or kisses.

CHAPTER 15
THE WINTER OF DISCONTENT

Flames danced lazily over a bed of glowing coals in the fireplace, giving off cozy warmth and soft, flickering, orange light. Emmett sat on their bed, bleary-eyed. He was drunk. Chris was standing and they were talking; or rather, she talked in harsh, angry tones. When Emmett attempted to speak at all, he could manage only a few slurred words. Their boys were sitting quietly on the floor out of the line of fire. As the conversation progressed, their parents' voices grew harsher. Then, with fire in her eyes and an angry scowl etching her face, Chris blurted out, "Well, I'm leaving!"

She dressed Gene and Charlie in their snowsuits, mittens, caps with ear flaps tied under their chins, thick socks, shoes and rubber goulashes. She threw on her overcoat, took Gene and Charlie by the hand and marched out the front door and into that cold winter night in early 1943. Whether too drunk or uncaring or both, Emmett did not try to stop her. These images were seared into Charlie's three-and-a-half year old memory from that very moment. Gene, being so much older, had much more seared into his, and the effects on him had begun to show.

Chris and her boys walked the block and a half to Ruth Morris's house, a gray two-story on Grayland Avenue on the corner across the street from John B. Cary Elementary School. Ruth lived there alone. Evelyn had already moved out and had her own place on Grove Avenue. Perk had been drafted and was in the Army at that time.

Though she returned home the next day, that incident deepened the fracture in the dam that held back the rising flood of discontent between Chris and Emmett. Within two months of that incident, on April 27, 1943, Chris would leave him forever. She filed for divorce, and a separation decree was issued on June 10 of that same year. Emmett did not oppose it except for visitation rights, an argument which he lost.

At that time, Virginia law required a two-year wait before a final divorce decree could be entered. In the interim, the couple was legally still married. The General Assembly did not want marriages to be thrown away out of anger or a passing disagreement. If it must end, it was best if done only after thoughtful, sober deliberation. The two-year wait was mandated in hope that reconciliation would save some marriages.

That waiting period was followed by a final divorce decree in mid-spring, 1945, which Emmett also did not oppose. The decree ordered him to continue to pay $40 per month (about eight percent of his pre-tax wages) in child support, and gave sole custody of the children to Chris, but it did not restore visitation rights to him.

Emmett's lack of visitation rights was due to his drinking and violent behavior. He never hit Chris or the boys, but in a fit of rage he would break and throw things. The judge figured Emmett would one day do physical harm to one of them, at least accidentally, and there was the almost certain emotional harm to the kids.

To his credit, while Emmett had no visitation rights, he was faithful in paying the court-ordered child support, even though his leftover income was barely enough for him to get by on. Chris neither asked for nor was awarded alimony. She wanted nothing from him for herself.

The marriage that had started out so promising had come to an unhappy end. It was her fourth shattering blow, following her family's loss of job and home in Richmond, and the deaths of her father and her beloved Edythe. Instead of crumbling under the weight of it all, Chris emerged from that crucible stronger, more resilient more self-reliant and more determined than ever. She had little tolerance for those she called "triflin." To her it was shameful, even disgraceful, for anyone to freeload on the backs of others who had to work for what they had. She disliked the very idea of government welfare. She, like every other self-respecting American, considered it morally wrong for anyone who was able to work to collect welfare.

At the same time, though, Christine had a soft heart for anyone who suffered an injury or loss beyond their control, or who was unfairly treated. Other people's misfortune brought tears to her eyes, and mistreatment could bring both tears and fire. While she felt sorry for the unfortunate, she had no patience with self-pity by anyone. The way she saw it, anyone who got knocked down by life should just get back up and make the best of it. Her attitude was partly the way her mind was wired and partly what she had experienced as a child. It made for strong character, but the downside was that she was not particularly nurturing. She loved babies, but once a child was past the tender years, she had little patience for whining and crying. Even so she was consumed with compassion for the sick, especially if they were also left destitute, and doubly if they were children of tender years. One of her favorite sayings was, "With a little common sense, you can figure out how to do just about anything you set your mind to." That attitude had a lot to do with what she would come to accomplish in life.

After her separation, Chris and her boys lived for a short time with Ruth on Grayland Avenue, just until things settled down and she found a rental house. Then they lived for a short time on Patterson Avenue in the west end. The house was a free-standing, small cottage, like a converted carriage house.

One night, while living there on Patterson, the air raid sirens started wailing, waking up the whole house. Charlie was terrified that Nazi airplanes were coming to drop bombs on them. He scrambled out of his crib and ran as fast as his little bare feet would carry him to his mommy's darkened bedroom. He jumped up on the bed and into the safety of her arms.

She pulled the covers over him, cuddled him and reassured him everything was alright. After he settled down, she reached up and raised the blackout shade covering the window behind the headboard and peeked outside. Charlie begged her not to open the shade because Nazis might be outside in the yard and would see her. She assured him there were no Nazis out there, and Charlie was soon sleeping peacefully again.

Behind that house on Patterson was a sapling tree, its trunk about one and half inches in diameter and tapered to a twig at the top. Somehow, Gene discovered that when he pulled it over and let it go, it would fly straight back up with considerable force. Since it is better to apologize later than to ask in advance when you know the answer will be no, Gene stripped the fledgling branches off of it. Then he used a knife that he snuck out of the kitchen to carve a shallow, spoon-like hollow at the top of the now-stripped trunk.

He then picked up a few small rocks from the alleyway and returned to the tree. As Charlie and some neighbor kids watched, Gene pulled the tree over, placed a rock on the spoon-shaped hollow he had carved and let go of the trunk. To the surprise and delight of both Gene and the other kids, the rock hurtled away in a long arc that carried it well into the front yard.

Gene had made a working catapult! He loaded and fired that thing several more times, with all the other kids getting a turn at putting a pebble on it. Finally, it was Charlie's turn, but he was not content to let Gene hold the sapling trunk down. He picked a rock bigger than any of the others, then pulled the sapling over with Gene's help. Once the tree was horizontal, Charlie insisted he could hold it and Gene let go. Holding the sapling with one hand, Charlie reached out with the other to put his outsized rock on the spoon-like spot. It was too big. He tried to balance it, but suddenly his grip on the sapling slipped, the rock fell to the ground, and the sapling sprang up and smacked him right in the nose.

Blood spattered, Charlie let out a yelp, the other kids screamed and Charlie started wailing. Gene, ever the calm one, took it all in with an I-told-you-so expression. Aunt Elizabeth, Henry's wife, who was sitting Gene and Charlie, came running outside to see what all the fuss was about. Now Elizabeth, though she was a diminutive woman, did not put up with foolishness, and she was not in the least sympathetic to Charlie. She took him by the ear into the house and scolded him the whole time she was packing his nostrils with cotton, washing the blood off his face and putting a fresh tee shirt on him. When Chris came home from work that afternoon, she listened as Elizabeth related the story, then the two of them went outside and managed to uproot Gene's catapult. That, of course, displeased him greatly, and he let his little brother know that he was to blame.

The place on Patterson Avenue was way too small to live in for an extended period of time, so Chris soon set about finding a more permanent home for herself and the boys. In a twist of irony, the house Chris found and rented was on Idlewood Avenue, diagonally across from the house she had walked out of when she left Emmett. It was just a half-block west of John B. Cary Elementary School and two doors west of the corner grocery story.

The house was one of those two story shoebox affairs that had been converted into two flats. The foyer had been partitioned off and a second entry door installed, leading to the staircase to the upper level. Chris had the downstairs. Chris painted the walls with pale blue water-based paint. The floors were painted with brown floor enamel, which was the standard thing to do to dress up the unfinished wood floors typical of that time. She also bought a large piece of linoleum to put on the kitchen floor under her white enamel, metal kitchen table.

She made the place as clean and nice as she could, but she could never get completely rid of the rats that infested the whole street. All in all, her new home was livable and even cozy. The exception to that was when a hard winter cold would freeze the exposed sewage drain and fresh water line, which had been retrofitted to run up the outside wall of the house. When that happened, she used a gasoline-fueled blowtorch to thaw the exposed pipes.

CHAPTER 16

BRASS, DUCKS AND WATER

Chris's income from the Bond Bread job was adequate, but finding a better-paying job was always on her mind. After she and Emmett split, she began looking for other "war work" that paid more. She had job skills at waiting tables, baking pies and cakes, driving a light delivery truck, making clothes, being a housewife and doing any sort of farm work. The pay from those jobs barely made ends meet. There was no room for any unexpected expense. Even so, her one powerful asset was that she believed in herself and in her ability to learn just about anything if given the chance.

On her bread route was a gasoline filling station and repair shop on Lakeside Avenue at the corner of Dumbarton Road. The rather large sign on the building read, in all bold letters, "Dick Mahle Service" (pronounced like "mail"). Naturally enough, the owner's name was Richard Mahle, but he preferred to be called Dick. That business was on Chris's regular route, and she used it as a staging site where she could off-load empty bread trays and pick up more loaves. She had already developed a first- name acquaintance with the owner.

Mahle was from Cleveland, Ohio, but he described his ancestry as Pennsylvania Dutch. That really meant he was of German stock, but with the war on and anti-German sentiment running high, it was prudent to use that colloquialism. Mahle had served as an aircraft engine mechanic in the US Army Air Corps during World War I. His assignment was at Langley Field in Hampton, Virginia. Following "The War to End All Wars," he settled in Richmond and opened his auto repair and filling station business there in Lakeside.

His shop had five work bays in addition to the wash bay and hydraulic lift bay. Otherwise, it was typical of filling stations at the time. The floors were black with a mix of dirt, oil and grease. The front counter sales area was dusty, dirty and carried a film of oil on everything, and the bathrooms were less than inviting. Mahle and the only other employee looked a lot like the shop floor. They fit the image of a "grease monkey." They wore khaki uniforms that seemed to be dirty most of the time.

On one of Chris's bread delivery trips to Lakeside she made her regular stop at Mahle's business. In the window was a Help Wanted sign. She went inside and spoke to the gas pump jockey in the office. "Is Mr. Mahle around?"

'Yes, Ma'am, he's in the back." The jockey went to the shop doorway and called out, "Hey, Dick!

"Yeah," shouted Mahle.

"The Bond Bread lady is here. She says she wants to talk to you."

"I'll be right up," Mahle shouted back. Moments later he walked into the office, wiping grease off his hands with a shop rag.

"Hi ya girl," he greeted Chris cheerily. "What can I do for you today? Hope I'm not in trouble."

"I see you have a Help Wanted sign in your window," Chris said. "Is the job still open?"

Mahle answered, "Yes it is, as a matter of fact. Why, do you know somebody looking for a job?"

"Yes, me," Chris replied matter-of-factly.

Mahle laughed good-naturedly, as if her remark was a joke.

"I'm not kidding. What does the job involve?" she asked.

"The job involves pumping gas, cleaning windshields, checking water, oil, tire pressure, antifreeze and battery levels, changing oil and filter, greasing suspension joints and steering fittings, washing and waxing cars, cleaning up the shop and tools at the end of every workday, mopping the shop floor with solvent every week, keeping the office and waiting area clean and cleaning the bathrooms - and that's just to start. Do you even know what a battery looks like or where to put the oil in a car motor, or where to drain it out?" he asked, a hint of sarcasm coloring his voice.

With slight exaggeration, Chris answered, "I was raised in the country. I've done most of those things, and what I don't know you can show me."

Mahle could see she wasn't kidding. He continued, "After you've learned all that stuff you'll have to learn to dismount tires, fix flats, re-mount and balance them, drain, flush and refill radiators with antifreeze, remove and replace batteries. And if that ain't enough, you'll have to learn how to pull cars out of ditches, hook up a tow chain; and, oh-by-the-way, the place is open from 7:00 a.m. to 8:00 p.m. seven days a week, including all holidays and Sundays. It's no job for sissies. You'll have to do all the work as good as a man. Do you think you can handle all that?"

Mahle's litany might have been intended to dissuade her, but it didn't. Chris never blinked. She looked him dead in the eyes and asked, "How much is the pay?"

Mahle was assertive, sometimes overbearing, a bit of a bully, very confident, and cussed a little. He paused a moment, then, with a dismissive wave of his hand, he turned to walk away, saying, "A skinny little girl like you couldn't handle the job."

He was either testing her determination or just being rudely dismissive. Either way, Mahle really and truly had no idea what kind of woman he was talking to. He soon learned that she was slightly more stubborn than he. He ruffled her feathers for sure, but rather than wilting under his insults or getting in his face, Chris stifled her temper and, with a grin and a twinkle in her eye, simply said, "Give me a chance, and I'll show you. If you're right you can fire me."

He stopped, turned, thought for a moment, and said, "I won't make allowances just because you're a woman. You'll wear work pants, shirt and shoes like the rest of us grease monkeys; no heels, no skirts, no open neckline blouses . . . and no long hair getting tangled in fan belts."

Chris: "Fine."

Mahle: "The pay is by the hour. No show, no pay.

"Fine, how many hours can I work?"

"As many as you want," said Mahle, a bit surprised, "if there is work to do."

She asked, "What's the rate?"

He: "Seventy-five cents an hour."

She stared at him, he at her, both silent.

Finally, Mahle blinked: "To start."

Chris smiled. She knew she had won the mental game.

"And then?" she asked.

Mahle: "We'll see."

She: "You say I have to do the job as well as a man. If I do, I want the same pay."

He smiled and laughed good-naturedly. He liked her brass. "OK, but only if you show me you can learn everything I told you and if you can do the whole job as good as a man, and I do mean IF," he said, his thick, calloused index finger with grease under the nail stabbing the air.

"We'll see. When can I start?"

He: "As soon as you're ready."

Chris: "I need to give my boss at Bond Bread a couple of weeks' notice. I owe him that."

He: "That's decent of you. Then we'll start you two weeks from today, OK?"

She: "Yes, I'll be here at 7:00 a.m. two weeks from today."

Mahle turned and walked away, muttering "This is probably a big mistake." Even so he recognized that having a pretty attendant on the pumps might be good for business.

Chris's brass paid off, and his "big mistake" turned out to be a remarkable success. To his credit, Mahle was an outstanding mechanic and an able and patient instructor. He showed her how to do the tasks in the Phase-1 job description that she didn't already know. She was like the duckling that discovered it was designed to live in water. In short order, Chris became a crackerjack filling station attendant.

Once she had settled into the job, Chris saw to it that both bathrooms at the station were as spotlessly clean as any person would want their own home to be, and the office area was rearranged to make space for a real customer lounge. The lounge area was supplied with current magazines, including some for the ladies, a jukebox and a radio. Eventually, a TV set was added. The wall calendar with photos of skimpily clad, big-busted pin-up girls was replaced with a more family-friendly one.

The plate glass windows of the customer lounge were regularly washed inside and out. All merchandize displays were kept stocked at all times and dusted as often as necessary to look fresh. The red Coca Cola cooler that used refrigerated water to cool the bottled drinks was drained and washed regularly.

In the office and lounge area, the floors were swept daily and washed frequently. In the shop bays, the floors were swept and wiped clean of grease and oil every evening at 5:00 p.m. when the repair shop closed and were periodically washed with solvent so customers and employees would not track grease and oil into the office, lounge or customers' cars. Tools were cleaned in solvent and put away every day. Outside, Chris planted flowers in the soil along the edge of the concrete apron, which she swept and hosed down to remove any petroleum spills.

She also convinced Mahle to provide enough uniforms for all employees to have a clean one twice a week and to have the uniform company wash and iron them. These were khaki tan, long-sleeved shirts with flap pockets and matching work pants. An Amoco oil company patch was sewn above one of the two shirt pockets, and the employee's name was embroidered above the other. The uniforms resembled the US Army standard-issue khaki uniform and were custom fitted for each employee.

This meant that Chris wore pants with the zipper in the front rather than on the hip, as was standard for women's slacks at that time. This proved to be shocking to a few of the customers, but Chris could not be bothered with all that. They soon got over it. Several customers complimented the appearance and cleanliness of the station and its employees, and especially remarked about how refreshing it was to have someone like Chris working there, and how she remembered their names and always seemed glad to see them.

Mahle was happy to hear those kinds of reports and always thanked the customer. Giving direct compliments to an employee, however, was not frequent. Maybe he thought giving a compliment would lead to the employee asking for a raise. One afternoon during a lull in customer traffic, he and Chris were standing in front of the entry door taking in the afternoon sun and mild temperatures. Mahle was in a rather mellow, relaxed mood. He talked for a while about the progress of repair jobs in the shop and the next days work. It seemed to Chris there was something else on his mind that he had not yet mentioned.

At a pause in the talk, Mahle broke out a pack of his favorite, "Kool," cigarettes, tapped one out and put it in his mouth to light, then extended the pack to Chris. Though she was not a smoker, she accepted the offer and let him light it up after he lit his own.

He took a long drag, then, without looking at her said, "I think you're gonna be OK working here. The place looks nice, you're good at the pumps and the customers seem to like you."

Chris, emulating his relaxed, off-the-cuff tone, took a drag on her cigarette and exhaled without inhaling. "Thanks. Does that mean I get a raise?"

Mahle chuckled, turned his head toward her and said with a grin, "Well, I said you're OK and can stay, but what's this stuff about a raise?" He thought for a few seconds, then, still not looking at her, said in a more serious tone, "If you think you're ready to start learning the real work, the mechanical stuff in the shop, and if you can handle that, we'll see about a raise."

"Alright," Chris replied. "When do we start?"

Mahle turned to her again and said, "Talk about being in a hurry. OK, we'll start tomorrow."

CHAPTER 17

THE ASCENT OF EVEREST

A t that time, there were none of the hydraulic machines that remove and install tires on rims. Changing a tire was done by muscle power alone, using two steel bars with flattened ends to pry the lip of a tire over the rim of the wheel, and a rubber mallet to pound the tire the rest of the way. Then an inner tube was stuffed inside the tire, the stem pushed through a hole in the wheel, the lip on the other side of the tire pried over the rim and the tube inflated.

Chris already knew how to change a tire. She learned that on the farm in Fluvanna. In the process of getting really good at it, however, she developed strong arms and a handshake that could make most men wince. Of course, she was too ladylike to do that to anyone . . . well, almost anyone. Exceptions were made for the deserving.

Lubricating a car was another matter. Back in that day cars did not have sealed suspension and steering joints. Instead, the joints between those parts had grease fittings, and grease had to be injected into them every thousand miles. Cars and light trucks had between nine and fourteen of these fittings. Every brand had a different number of fittings and they were in different places.

Since the station was an independent shop, Chris had to know the fittings of all brands of cars and light trucks. Changing the oil and filter was much the same, and the number of quarts required to refill an engine varied too. She quickly mastered all of these tasks and was eager to take on more.

The novelty of a pretty, young woman working in an auto service and repair shop, and doing "a man's work" as well as the men, drew the attention of the Richmond newspapers. A second newspaper story about Chris was published, focusing on her skill as a service station attendant. A photo of her mounting a tire on a rim appeared with the story. When the paper came out, Mahle brought it to the station and bragged to customers all day about Chris.

At closing time that night, just before everyone left for home, Mahle said, "Let's have a shot and toast Chris's newspaper story." He produced a fifth of whiskey and several small Dixie cups from under the counter. Chris took a cold bottle of 7-Up from the red Coca-Cola cooler, dried the water from it with a shop rag and opened it. Each of the several employees and Mahle received two cups, one containing about an ounce of whiskey, the other filled with 7-Up.

Raising his two cups, Mahle said, "Here's to Chris's newspaper story. It's good for business!" Everyone laughed and downed their shot followed by the 7-Up, then lit up a cigarette.

As time went by and the business grew, that became a daily ritual, with Chris going along with "the boys," so she would fit in and be accepted. A few folks around those parts thought it was improper or "un-ladylike" for a woman to work in such a place. Still, most people saw it as the result of the wartime labor shortage and accepted it as a sign of the times.

Word of mouth and the newspaper story soon set the business humming. Women customers were flocking in as much as admiring men. It wasn't long before more help was needed. As the business grew, so did Chris's appetite for learning. Her boss and the other mechanics were willing to teach her, and her knowledge grew rapidly, along with her pay. She readily grasped and quickly mastered everything she learned and eventually became more skilled than the men at just about anything involving repairing cars and light trucks.

Chris became equally comfortable with rebuilding brake systems, power steering, fuel and electrical systems, manual and automatic transmissions; grinding, polishing and adjusting engine valves, replacing pistons and rings, boring cylinders, total rebuilding any six-or eight-cylinder engine, adjusting and rebuilding carburetors, setting the engine timing, rebuilding electrical distributors and total tune-ups.

She later expanded both her skills and the business to include installing new upholstery, straightening body dents, replacing body panels, sanding, priming and painting, and on and on. She had a natural talent for it and eventually excelled at every kind of automotive repair. A key talent in many engine repair jobs was diagnosing the causes of a problem in the first place. This was especially true when engine problems were caused by a combination of several different things.

Where Chris really became a celebrity in the auto repair industry around Richmond was in diagnosing those unusual mechanical and electrical problems, and jobs that called for a delicate touch such as spray painting, adjusting carburetors, setting engine timing, grinding and polishing valves and valve seats, adjusting valves, setting up and adjusting distributors and adjusting automatic transmissions. Chris was so good at those jobs that service department managers at some of the factory dealerships would have a car towed to her for diagnosis and repair when their own factory-trained mechanics could not figure out a problem.

A third newspaper story was done about Chris during the prime of her career. That one focused on how advanced and diversified her knowledge and skill was. Chris actually completed professional schools to become a Certified Master Mechanic in automatic and manual transmissions, electrical systems and fuel systems.

Her work also included operating a service truck, which was a pickup with tow-chains, a tow bar and a wide, steel bumper on the front. When she went out to retrieve a car in a ditch or stuck in mud or snow, she could often just drive the car out without using the truck except to get to its location. When she couldn't do that, she could often get a car out and back on the road with just the pickup truck when others would think a wrecker was needed.

Chris had found a career niche that was unique for her time and which met her need for validation. She felt fulfilled, pleased that she was doing something worthwhile and doing it exceptionally well, and she clearly transformed that business into a model of what a clean, inviting, professional repair shop could be.

The one drawback to her success was her long hours. She worked from 7:00 a.m. to 8:00 p.m. every day for the first several years on the job. Her initial pay scale brought her $68 per week, far better than she could have made at any traditional woman's job. After that her pay rate went up, and she could make more with fewer hours. She and Mahle arranged it so that six days a week he opened at 7:00 and went home at 5:00, while Chris came in at 10:00 in the morning and worked through to closing at 8:00. On Sundays, he went to church, and it was left to Chris to open at 8:00 and close at 7:00. The reduction in work hours did not carry a pay cut, but it wasn't much help as far as time with her boys was concerned.

CHAPTER 18
LITTLE RASCALS

An old saying observes that trouble comes in threes. At home alone and after dark, with their mother at work and the sitter gone, two little boys proved that old saying to be true, and they were just being boys doing what boys do.

Caper One - "Uh Oh!"

Though her job at the station was in the Henrico County neighborhood of Lakeside, Chris and her boys continued to live in the rented "shotgun" house on Idlewood Avenue.

Chris enrolled Gene in kindergarten and Charlie in daycare at St. Andrews Episcopal Church, located down Idlewood Avenue at Laurel Street. For Charlie's first grade year and Gene's second, they went to William Fox Elementary. Although John B. Cary Elementary was only a half-block away from where they lived, Chris's boys went to Fox, much further away, but still within walking distance. That was because Fox had daycare after school on weekdays and Saturdays for working mothers.

The program was staffed by teachers and included supervised playtime in the schoolyard as well as lunch, a nap, an afternoon snack during weekdays and lunch on Saturday. The daycare center operated late enough for parents on a normal work schedule to pick up their children after work, but Chris's schedule was not normal.

At 7:45 p.m. Chris and whoever else was working would start bringing in the outdoor items and displays such as tire inventory, water cans, windshield cleaner dispensers, paper towel dispensers, trash cans, the air hose and so on. Closing all the windows and doors, doing the cash count and running the cash register totals would take more time, then she had to drive the six or so miles home. She was often not home before 8:20.

When her boys were little, they walked home after school at Fox Elementary and were met by a sitter, usually a teenaged son or daughter of one of Chris's friends. But there were more than a few times when they were home alone until Chris came home. You're probably thinking two grade-school boys like Gene and Charlie, at home alone after school, just might get into a little mischief ... and they did. They both believed that their mother was telepathic and would find out exactly what they had done, but if you were a child once you know that never kept two little rascals from any fun mischief their imaginative minds could cook up.

On one occasion, when Gene was in second grade, Charlie in first, they were home alone in the gap between when the sitter had to leave and Chris arrived home. The boys had the radio turned up loud and were running around the house whooping and hollering and playing tag. After a while the next door neighbor yelled at them to quiet down or he'd call the cops . . . so the boys naturally cranked the radio up louder and kept right on whooping it up. He was a crotchety old sour puss, always complaining about something, mostly them.

After a little while, Gene, being bigger, half-a-head taller, older and more perceptive than his younger brother, figured they'd best turn it down. They did, then sat quietly listening to shows like Sky King, Roy Rogers, Gene Autry, or maybe Sergeant Preston of the

Yukon, or even Fibber Magee and Molly. Soon, they heard a car pull up out front. Instead of hearing one door open and close, there were two. They looked out the window.

"Uh oh," said Gene.

His smart decision to turn the radio down had been just a tad too late. Two policemen came to the door and rang the bell. To the boys, they looked like giants. The officers were both slender, but one was a little shorter than the other, and they had real guns and badges, and handcuffs and night sticks too. Charlie was so scared he had a strong urge to pee. Gene, ever the cool head, not so much.

The taller policeman said in a big, bossy voice, "There's been a complaint about noise - a radio too loud - at this address. Are your parents home?"

Gene spoke up: "No, Sir. Mommy's at work and Daddy don't live here."

Officer: "What have you boys been doing?"

Gene: "Nuthin'," just lis'nin' tuh the radio."

"Has the radio been as loud the whole time as it is now?" the shorter cop asked in a nicer tone.

"Oh, yes, Sir," Gene lied, as Charlie enthusiastically nodded and put on his best wide-eyed, innocent look.

The shorter officer turned to the other one and said he didn't think it was loud enough to complain about. The taller one agreed and warned Gene and Charlie to keep it quiet. The policemen left, and the boys laughed themselves silly that they had fooled the cops.

Caper Two - The Fire Dance

Soon after that evening, Chris's boys were home alone in the gap once again. It was after dark and they were playing ring-and-run up and down Idlewood Avenue and at least one or two streets over. They got away with that a lot, and it was great fun. Their success emboldened them. They added a wrinkle that might have pushed the game just a little bit too far. They got out a brown paper lunch bag, and one of them pooped in it. Then they snuck out and sat it on a neighbor's porch, lit the bag on fire, rang the doorbell and bounded back to their house like two rambunctious puppies.

I'll bet you already know which neighbor it was, right? Yeah, that's the one. They watched as the crotchety old man opened the door, rushed out onto the porch and started stomping the fire out. He looked like an Indian in the movies doing the fire dance. When he realized what was all over his shoes, in his shoes, on his pants and porch, the boys could not keep from giggling no matter how hard they tried. The giggling turned into out-of-control laughing and rolling on the floor 'til their ribs hurt and their eyes watered.

The grumpy neighbor figured it had to be Gene and Charlie, so he just naturally had to rat them out. Soon, two police officers pulled up in front of the house and got out of their car. Gene and Charlie ran and hid under Chris's bed for a hasty strategy meeting. Charlie said, "I got ah idea: let's hide here, an' not answer th' door, an' maybe they'll go way!"

Gene said, "That won't work, Dope. All th' lights are on and the radio's playin'. The cops'll know somebody's home."

Charlie said, "What're we gonna do? I don' wanna go to jail."

Gene, always the cool one, said, "We'll answer the door and play like we didn't do it."

Seconds later the policemen rang, but the boys didn't run. Gene opened the door. It was the same two policemen, and they looked really mad. Charlie figured they would remember Gene and him from before. He just knew they were going to jail. This time the two policemen walked right into the house. They wanted to know the boys' names, their mother's name, where she worked and whether they put poop in a bag and lit it on fire on the next-door neighbor's porch.

The boys put on their innocent faces again and gave an honest answer to every question except the last one. "No Sir, we don't know nothin' about that," they said, wagging their wide-eyed heads from side to slide.

Their innocent look wasn't working this time. The policemen pressed the interrogation, bending down and glaring into the frightened boys' faces. "We know you did it. You might as well admit it," the tall one demanded, his eyes glaring and his brows scrunched together.

Charlie was about to cry and confess that Gene did it and made him go along, when Chris walked up onto the porch. *Saved!* Charlie thought.

You might say Chris was a little more than curious about what Gene and Charlie had been up to. "What's the problem, officer? I'm Chris Payne, their mother," she said.

"Evening, Ma'am," said the short one. I'm Officer Dodd. My partner here is Officer Finch. Headquarters received a call from one of your neighbors, who reported that someone had filled a paper bag with . . . uh . . . uuuh"

"Doodoo," said Officer Finch, obviously embarrassed.

"Yeah, then whoever did it set fire to it on the porch next door," continued Officer Dodd.

Finch added, "Yes, Ma'am, and he, I mean the complainant, thinks your boys here did it, Ma'am."

Chris listened attentively. When the officers finished, she looked sternly at Gene and Charlie for a moment and read the guilt on their faces like a flashing neon sign. She turned to the policemen, gave them a knowing look and replied in a friendly, cooperative tone, "Thank you, officers. I think I understand the situation. It seems you have two choices here. You can cuff these two and take them down to the jail for further questioning, or you can let me get to the bottom of it my way."

Chris, the two policemen, Gene and Charlie, all knew right then what Chris meant by "get to the bottom." Chris's boys thought it would have been better if the cops had taken them to jail.

Officer Dodd said, "Well, the complainant did say he never saw who actually did it, so I believe it would be OK this once not to arrest these two boys, and to let you handle it instead."

He looked at Officer Finch, who nodded his assent and added, "Yes, I think that's appropriate. But mind you," he said, turning to look at the boys in a fake expression of anger, "if anything like this *ever* happens again, we'll know it was you, and it'll be off to jail with the both of you."

The officers said good night, tipped their hats to Chris and left. Chris thanked them, shood the boys into the house, closed the door firmly behind her, locked the dead bolt and turned slowly toward them. Off came her belt, and off went Gene and Charlie, running for dear life. Their house had a hallway leading from the front door all the way through to the kitchen at the back of the house. To the right of the entry was a living room connected by French doors to a dining room, which Chris used for her bedroom, and a door from that room back to the hallway making a more-or-less circular layout.

Gene and Charlie ran from the entry hall through the living room, through Chris's bedroom, then down the hall and back to the living room. Round and round they went, with Chris in hot pursuit, belt in hand. After a few laps, Chris ducked behind a door and waited for them to come around again. As Gene and Charlie ran passed, she jumped out, and they crashed right into her. That's when she got to the bottom of things. She gave them a whippin' that neither of their bottoms ever forgot.

Chris's boys knew that a whippin' was the same thing as a "lickin'," but they didn't know where the word lickin' came from. That night they found out. With the buckle end of a belt wrapped around her hand, the opposite end dangling down looked a little like a long tongue. When that tongue slapped across their legs and fanny hard enough to sting and even leave a pink mark, you could say the belt "licked" them.

Caper Three - In the Name of Science

Gene and Charlie were home alone again and just a little bored. Gene decided to do a chemistry "experiment" in the living room. He mixed a few household chemicals together in a small bottle and added some of Chris's perfume and a little of her rubbing alcohol. He shook it up real good and put a kitchen match to it to see if it would burn . . . and it did. Oh boy, did it burn.

The flame was so big it scared the daylights out of both of them. Gene started blowing the flame as hard as he could, but it didn't do any good. Then he started waving the burning bottle around, trying to get the fire to go out. Instead of going out, the burning liquid splashed out and onto the seat cushion of an upholstered chair and the rug it was sitting on. Now he had three fires.

With the fires small but growing fast, Charlie was pretty sure it was time to leave; but Gene, being a pretty smart kid, put the lid on the burning bottle, turned over the burning chair cushion, which smothered the flames and hid the hole in the cushion. Then he stomped out the burning rug and pulled the chair over to cover the hole. Like I said, Gene was a smart kid.

Chris didn't find out about Gene's "experiment" for a good long time - until the day she decided to rearrange furniture. The chair was moved, the hole in the rug was found. After some pointed questions, Gene confessed, sort of. "Me an' Charlie were doin' some chemical stuff, an' lit it, an' some of it got on the rug," he explained. This time, however, Charlie had nothing to do with it.

Before Gene could say anything more, Chris flipped the cushion and found the as-yet unmentioned burn-hole in it. You're probably thinking she blew a fuse. Well, she was plenty mad, but at first she stayed calm and told them how dangerous it was to play with fire, and how lucky they were that they didn't burn the house down with them inside it. That's when her fuse blew and she gave them another painful lesson. The boys deserved all the whippings they _got_. . . but they didn't get all they _deserved_. Charlie didn't deserve that one, but he figured it made up for one of the times he didn't get one he deserved.

Being on their own after school without adult supervision, the boys were quickly turning feral. For errant incidents that were dangerous, destructive or malicious they needed correction that they would not forget and would not want to repeat. Chris's corrections gave both boys a healthy respect for her authority, a clear understanding of right and wrong, and an even clearer understanding that doing wrong has swift and unpleasant consequences.

CHAPTER 19

PEACE COMES HOME

B y 1945, Ruth had returned to farm life, but in a different place. She rented a farmhouse just outside of Richmond on Sadler Road, about a mile off Broad Street Road. It sat smack in the middle of a flat, wide open wheat field. The place was two-stories, Victorian style, with a "T" layout, tin roof, white siding and a large front porch with gray floor and blue ceiling. The shed-roofed kitchen on the back of the house was added well after the house was built. The door opening from dining room to kitchen was only six feet high. When Henry was there he had to duck every time he went through it.

In August that summer the war was finally won. Germany had surrendered in May, Japan in August. After just a few days, the government announced an end to gasoline rationing. The station was open, and Chris, Dick Mahle, another attendant, plus Gene and Charlie, were present when the broadcast came over the airwaves, right at the beginning of the evening rush hour.

At Chris's urging, Mahle decided to sell gas without ration coupons right then. Chris sent her boys out to the street to spread the word. Gene was assigned to the corner of Lakeside and Dumbarton, Charlie was posted to the other end of the station's frontage on

Lakeside Avenue. They both began shouting to all the passing mo-
torists, "Gas without coupons! Gas without coupons! Come fill up!"

Almost immediately, cars were at every pump, and the line of
cars waiting to get gas stretched down the outside lane of Lakeside
Avenue for about a block. That night, they sold all the gas they
had – regular, medium and high-test, every drop gone.

It was well past the regular closing time when Mahle, Chris, her
boys and the other station attendant dragged themselves home.
Everyone, including Gene and Charlie, though tired, was elated.
Not only had they made a lot of money for the station, they got the
jump on all the other stations on Lakeside Avenue, and had helped
many Lakeside families. This resulted in a surge of new customers
for the station.

A couple of months after that, Perk came home for good. Gene
and Charlie were at Ruth Morris's farm when Perk arrived in uniform, carrying a duffle bag filled with clothes, personal effects
and war souvenirs. Charlie took particular delight in playing with
Perk's souvenir German helmet and bayonet.

Chris's boys were all over him, grabbing him by the hands and
tugging at him, hanging on him when he was sitting down. They
wanted him to play. Perk, being good-natured and fond of his
nephews, was happy to oblige.

The only available bedroom for Perk to use was the small nursery or reading room directly above the front entry. In it was a
single-size, iron-framed bed built just like an army barracks bed,
with a thin army-like mattress. The bed was just what Perk had
used in the service.

The problem with both his army bunk and this bed was that his
feet and ankles hung off the end, even when the top of his head
was rubbing the head of the bed. Inevitably, his feet would come
out from under the covers during the night.

When Chris's boys stayed on their Granny Morris's farm, just
about every day Charlie was awakened by the smell of eggs, bacon,

biscuits and coffee wafting up from the kitchen, even before Ruth called out for everyone to wake up.

Charlie, in his pajamas and bare feet, would sneak down to Perk's room and tickle his protruding feet until Perk woke up. When he did, Perk would grab Charlie and drag him up onto the bed and play like he was some kind of growling monster ready to eat him up. He'd tickle Charlie and romp with him. Soon, Gene would come and join in the fun until they heard Granny call: "Gene, Charles Edward, Perkins time for you boys get washed up and come down for breakfast. You all come on now."

Looking back on those days long ago, it seems certain that Perk's return home, safe from the war, gave much-needed adult male attention to Chris's boys. As for Perkins himself, he seemed relaxed and enjoyed being Gene and Charlie's playmate. Outward appearances, however, concealed inner turmoil that he brought home from the war, turmoil that would soon surface.

Perk was living on his saved-up army pay and still hadn't taken a job yet, but he was a big help to Ruth on the farm. He made repairs, fed the animals and drove Ruth to the feed-and-seed store. He waited patiently while she looked at the colorful floral print patterns on feed sacks to find just the right one that would be made into a dress, skirt or blouse, when the sacks were emptied.

Perk finally got around to seeing just one girl. He talked about her often. Ruth asked if he was going to bring his girl around to meet his mother. One Saturday, Perk left the house in mid-morning, saying he had to run some errands. He returned in mid-afternoon, accompanied by the girl he had talked so much about. Chris's boys were there that weekend, so they got to see her.

"Mother," said Perk, "I'd like you to meet my girl, Jesse, Jesse Greer. Sweetheart, this is my mother, Ruth Morris."

Jesse said, in her soft, sweet, southern tone, "It's so nice to meet you, Mizz Morris. Perk has told me so much about you."

Ruth replied, "It's nice to meet you too, Jesse. You're about the only thing Perk talks about these days, so it's time we met."

Jesse was pretty as a picture, with milky skin, big, bright eyes, and long, dark hair. She was really nice to Gene and Charlie, and soft in all the right places. Charlie and Gene loved it when she grabbed them up and hugged them. Though Charlie was only six, he adored her.

Some months later, during one of Jesse's visits to the farm, Ruth, Perk, Jesse, Gene and Charlie were all sitting on the front porch. Ruth Morris was in her rocking chair, Jesse and Perk were on the glider, while Gene and Charlie were draped over the other chair listening while Perk and Granny did most of the talking.

Eventually, when the small talk came to a pause, Perk spoke up. "Well, Mother, I have some news. Jesse and I are getting married."

Ruth continued to rock for a long moment, then answered her youngest son calmly, matter-of-factly. "That's nice, Perkins. What are the two of you gonna live on? You don't have a job."

Perk, grinning broadly, a playful twinkle in his eyes, looked at Jesse, then at Ruth, and replied just as matter-of-factly, "Why, Mother, we'll live on luuv!"

Ruth parried, "Umm-hmm. I expect you all will get mighty hungry, presently."

Jesse, in her soothing, alto voice, said, "Perk will get a job, Mizz Morris. You don't need to be worried about that. And I have a job. We'll be alright."

"Well, I wish you both the best." said Ruth, signaling her acquiescence. She had made her point.

Jesse then leaned out of the glider, hugged Ruth and reassured her that they would be just fine.

Perk and Jesse soon tied the knot. Though they had their share of setbacks, mainly from Perk's troubles that many attributed to the war, that knot remained strong and tight for all the years of their long lives. Though never rich in earthly things, Perk and Jesse enjoyed an overflowing and enduring abundance of love. Their children can testify to that, as they saw it and were recipients of it.

CHAPTER 20
ENTER PRINCE CHARMING

Evelyn worked for a bakery in Richmond, not far from where Chris lived on Idlwood Avenue. Sometimes Chris and her boys dropped by the bakery to visit Evelyn. Usually it was evening when Chris was off work. Evelyn would be working the night shift, baking for the next day's business. On these visits, Evelyn would always give Chris some day-old pie or other pastry. Gene and Charlie, of course, thought they were scrumptious, and Chris let them eat it but not all in one sitting, of course.

Chris saw Evelyn less than she saw Henry but more than she did Perk. Evelyn was cheerful and warm. She fussed over Gene and Charlie just as she did Henry's children. Evelyn never had children of her own, but she enjoyed her nieces and nephews as often as she could.

One evening Chris was invited to visit Evelyn at her apartment on Monument Avenue. Evelyn was seeing a gentleman friend and wanted Chris and him to meet. For reasons unknown, Chris took Charlie with her. Gene didn't go because he was involved elsewhere doing something more fun. Charlie always liked visiting Aunt Evelyn, because she made over him – besides, she was his source of free desserts.

When Chris arrived with Charlie in tow, she was duly impressed with her sister's gentleman friend right from the introduction. Impeccably dressed in a very nice suit, he was six feet tall, trim, handsome with wavy hair, and spoke in a smooth, baritone voice. He was very polite, very polished. He was altogether charming and attractive. It was easy to see that Evelyn was strongly attracted to her gentleman friend, who preferred to be called William, not Bill or Will, just, William. Chris got the impression that the connection between the two was a serious thing. He was Evelyn's Prince Charming.

William was not naïve. He knew Evelyn's sister was there to size him up for her, and he did all the right things to impress Chris. He even played with Charlie, who enjoyed the playful attention of a grown man, just as he enjoyed his fun times with Uncle Perk. Charlie liked William, and William seemed to enjoy Charlie, who soon thought of William as a playmate.

After a while, energetic Charlie stepped on William's watch, which he had taken off and laid aside, and broke the crystal. He thought it was funny and laughed. William didn't think it was funny at all. His charming, proper-but-light-hearted, kid-loving personality turned instantly into something very different. Oops!

William came at him, angry and bellowing. He grabbed Charlie by the arms, shaking him so hard Charlie's teeth rattled. He squeezed Charlie's arm 'til it hurt, got in his face and berated him. It scared the wits out of the little guy, and he started to cry. Evelyn and Chris jumped up, grabbed William and pulled him away. Then William started shouting at Evelyn and Chris about Charlie, describing him, let's just say, in unflattering slang terms.

That was it. Evelyn and Chris ganged up on him, told him Charlie was just a child, he didn't mean any harm, and William should not take offense. Chris said she would pay for the watch repair. It was all to no avail. The guy ranted on and was soon calling

Evelyn and Chris ugly names. At that, Evelyn ordered him to leave. William ignored her and did not budge.

Chris had had enough of this Prince Charming. She straightened up, stepped forward and got face to face with him, her eyes blazing. She grabbed him by the wrist, dug in her nails and squeezed until he winced. William tried to pull his arm free but could not break her grip. When he realized that she was restraining him with one hand, he stopped his rant.

Chris spoke to him with an unmistakable, voice of authority. "My sister told you to leave. Now git!" She mustered her full five-foot-eight height and pushed him toward the door. The look in Chris's eye told William she meant to remove him by force if necessary. He stopped resisting, turned and left, slamming the door behind him.

Through his tears, Charlie said he was sorry and didn't mean to make William mad. He felt terribly guilty that he caused Aunt Evelyn to lose the man she thought she was going to marry. Chris told him that he should have behaved himself, but that it was OK anyway because William was not a very nice man. Evelyn grabbed Charlie up in her arms, hugged him to her bosom and said, "That's alright, Charlie. I'm glad to find out about William's other side sooner than later."

Chris and Evelyn speculated that if he was that abusive toward Charlie he would probably beat a child if he had one, and beat Evelyn too if she had married him. After thinking about it for a day, Charlie told his mom that maybe it's a good thing, because if he hadn't broken William's watch, Aunt Evelyn might have married a meanie. As it turned out, Evelyn never did marry, but she never regretted losing William either. She remained kind and happy, and affectionate to her nieces and nephews whenever a family affair brought her and them together.

CHAPTER 21

FRISBEES

Chris, her brother Henry and their families visited back and forth fairly regularly. Henry, who never gave up his fondness for growing crops, planted and tended a garden on a small plot of land near their house in the east end. From time to time he would bring Chris tall grocery bags filled with vegetables from his garden.

Usually, there would be two bags filled with fresh corn, green beans, butter beans, tomatoes, cucumbers, yellow squash, onions and more. Then, whenever something went wrong with Henry and Elizabeth's car, they would bring it to Chris, and she would repair it for free, or for the cost of parts only.

At Christmas, Henry's family exchanged gifts with Chris and her boys. They were never more than a handkerchief, a pair of socks or maybe a pair of knitted woolen gloves – just small, inexpensive things, but it was enough to say they recognized their family ties and valued them.

An exceptional social visit took place at Henry and Elizabeth's house when Chris and her boys were invited to a formal Easter dinner. Charlie was about 8, and Gene 10. That was a cause for dressing up. Henry and Elizabeth had two kids, Richard and Barbara. Juanita, their third, came later. Chris, of course, just had Gene and Charlie, who enjoyed being with Richard and Barbara when they could.

As Chris pulled up in front of Henry and Elizabeth's house, she reminded Gene and Charlie: "Now boys, when we sit down to eat, mind your manners. Wait for the blessing. Charlie, don't chew with your mouth open. Remember to say please and thank you, keep one hand in your lap, take small bites, don't drink your water with your mouth full and sit up straight."

Gene and Charlie replied in unison, and with resignation, "Yes, Ma'am."

Both leaves had been added to Elizabeth's dining room table, making the foot on one end stick out nearly into the next room. The table was dressed with a white linen tablecloth and neatly fold-ed matching napkins. Elizabeth's best flatware, china and glass-ware were all meticulously set. All the kids, washed up, combed and dressed in their Sunday best, were soon off by themselves, tak-ing their mind off of their awkwardness over the fancy clothes and shiny shoes. Chris busily lent a hand helping Elizabeth and Henry.

Soon, Elizabeth announced that all was ready. Henry turned and spoke to the four kids in his usual firm monotone and concise, clipped words. "Barbara. Richard. Charles Edward. Gene. Come on to the table now. It's time to eat."

After a short flurry of kids scrambling to their assigned chairs, all were seated around the elegantly-set dining room table. Henry, seated at the head of the table, bowed his head, giving the cue for all talking to stop and heads to bow. When all was quiet and still, he prayed, "Dear Lord, thank you for these gifts which we are about to receive from Thy bounty. Amen."

A subdued commotion erupted as serving dishes were passed, one to the other. Soon everyone's plate was filled and eating com-menced in earnest-with small bites, of course - amid amiable adult conversation. The children did not speak unless spoken to, in obser-vance of a long-time Victorian rule. Somewhere along the way, Chris missed out on the bread. There were hot rolls but also store-bought, sliced white bread. The bread platter was sitting on the table in front of Richard, who was next to his dad at the head of the table. Chris, sitting at the other end, called out to Richard in her usual light-hearted way, "Hey Richard, how about throwing me a slice of that loaf bread." Richard answered very politely, "Yes, Ma'am." He then picked up a single slice of bread and flipped it like a Frisbee down the length of the table. Elizabeth, seated nearest the kitchen door, gasped, and the kids watched in wide-eyed awe as the bread floated through the air, seemingly in slow motion. On it flew at two feet of altitude above the table top. The spongy, wobbling missile sailed over the candlesticks and was headed for a landing somewhere in the next room. As it passed overhead, Chris calmly reached up with one hand and deftly snatched it in mid-flight.

"Thank you, Richard," she said as she put the bread on her plate, then finished the sentence she had started. Everyone exhaled and broke out laughing; that is, everyone except Elizabeth.

She was aghast. Her son had embarrassed her in front of "company." She lit into Richard, scolding him sharply. Poor little Richard sitting there looking bewildered and a little frightened, didn't know what he had done wrong. Chris spoke up. "Don't be hard on him, Elizabeth. He only did what I asked him to do."

Henry, in his usual calm, soft-spoken way, interceded on Richard's behalf, gently smoothing Elizabeth's ruffled feathers, reminding her that they were all family, and that no harm was done. With decorum restored the dinner proceeded. When it was over, the kids, whose bellies were all well-rounded, were excused to go to another room to play. Of course, Chris hadn't meant for Richard to literally throw the bread, but it was natural for a child his age to take literally anything an adult said, and he had, quite literally, obeyed her. For Chris's part, she was a bit more judicious when giving instructions to the kids after that.

CHAPTER 22

DAMSELS, DUNGEONS AND OGRES

The boys' memories of Fox Elementary School are all warm. It was a wonderful school and they enjoyed their classmates and teachers. Charlie attended kindergarten and first grade at Fox; Gene, second and third. For reasons unknown to them, though, the boys were transferred to John B. Cary school the following September, in 1947. Maybe it was because Fox stopped its day care service, now that the war had ended and droves of working mothers were housewives again.

John B. Cary School was a very different place. To Charlie, the gray, neo-Gothic limestone building looked like a medieval castle, all dark and dingy. Some of the kids there acted like they were well on their way to becoming hoodlums. Charlie figured the castle must have a dungeon deep underneath where the hoodlums would end up.

Charlie has two good memories of John B. Cary School. One was that it was only a half-block from home, which eventually became very important to him. The other was Alice. She was a cute, blue-eyed girl, with curly blonde hair, who joined Charlie's second grade class for the spring semester. Soon after Charlie got to know her she told him she *liked* him! She even tried to hug him one day out on the playground. Charlie didn't know what to do because he wasn't used to being hugged by anybody except his Aunt Evelyn and Aunt Jesse, and he didn't see them that much. But Charlie liked Alice's hug a lot.

One day in class, Charlie shot a spitball at another boy through a straw he got from the cafeteria. It missed his target and skidded across the teacher's desk, stopping just short of her stomach. She made him sit in the punishment chair in the back of the room next to an upright piano. A short few minutes later, Alice intentionally misbehaved in front of the teacher. Naturally, she was sent to another punishment desk next to Charlie's. As soon as the teacher turned to the blackboard, Alice leaned over toward Charlie and whispered, "Let's go back there," pointing to the open space behind the piano. "You go first."

Charlie, being a boy, naturally did as the fair damsel bid. She quickly followed. Straight away, she took Charlie by the shoulders and whispered, "Be real quiet, OK?"

Charlie nodded as Alice put her finger to her mouth and quietly intoned, "Shhhhh." She then pulled him close and planted a kiss right on his lips. His first kiss! Then, she gave him her little bangle bracelet and said, "You can have this to remind you I'm your girlfriend."

Their romantic encounter soon ended when the teacher noticed the two empty punishment desks next to the piano. She called out to the miscreants, who quickly returned to their desks. They had to stay after class that day and write an "I will not . . ." sentence twenty times. In Charlie's mind that was a small price to pay to be kissed by Alice. He was certain she was the prettiest girl in the world. Alice's bangle bracelet was made of dingy, tarnished brass, but that didn't matter. Charlie treasured it like real gold. He even cut a hole in the plaster wall next to his upper-bunk bed just so he could have a safe place to keep it.

That hole in the wall was how Chris found out about Alice. Charlie hadn't realized that his tall mother would see the hole just walking by. The punishment Charlie got on account of that hole in the plaster didn't deter his affection for Alice one bit. He was, for the first time in his short life, "in luuv" with a girl. Why, he even began to think Cary Castle might be alright after all.

But alas, young Squire Charlie, smitten by the fair Damsel Alice, Princess of Cary Castle, was *noticed* by a big, roly-poly sixth-grader. Charlie was pretty sure he was the ogre that lived in the dungeon below the castle. On the playground during recess one day, the six-grader just came over and took the ball Alice and Charlie were playing with.

"That's our ball. We were playin' with it. Give it back," Charlie demanded.

"Nope," replied the ogre indifferently, as he continued to bounce the ball.

Charlie tried to intercept the ball in mid-bounce, but the ogre stiff-armed him in the face and pushed him away.

"Give it back!" Charlie demanded more insistently.

"Nope," repeated the ogre.

Squire Charlie looked at Princess Alice, who was standing there watching the whole thing. Charlie's ego lay in tatters on the ground. The big boy had shown him up to be the puny, helpless little twerp that he felt like, a wimp, who couldn't do anything to make the ogre give the ball back. What's worse, he did it in front of Princess Alice!

Squire Charlie did the only thing he could to redeem himself in Alice's eyes: he scrunched his eyebrows together and glared at the ogre. Then, with all the sarcasm he could muster, he bravely sneered, "You're a big, fat dummy! Fatty, fatty, bumba latty, can't get through the bathroom door!"

Enraged, the big sixth grader came lumbering after Charlie and started yelling cuss words and pushing him. Luckily for the bully, Charlie was saved when the school bell rang them back to class. Alice and Charlie bolted for the school door. The bully yelled after them that he'd be waiting for Charlie after school and would beat him to a pulp, and Charlie *be-leeeved* him.

That afternoon, for the first time, Charlie was not looking forward to school letting out. When it did, he tried really hard to sneak past the bully, but he was soon spotted. Charlie took off running, and the bully took off after him as fast as he could, which wasn't very fast. He looked about three times Charlie's size, but Charlie was pretty fast. After all, he had plenty of practice running.

Squire Charlie beat the ogre to the front door of his family fort, slammed it shut and turned the dead bolt just as the sixth-grade bully reached the porch. Charlie was standing in the entry hall looking through the beveled-glass pane when the ogre's round body bounced off the heavy oak door like a giant beach ball. Charlie said to himself, *"Boy, am I glad we live only a half of a block from school!"*

The ogre really looked scary the way he was staring at Squire Charlie through the glass. He tried to open the door but got nowhere, so he angrily ordered Charlie to unlock it. Charlie thought, *"He must think I'm as dumb as he is."*

Charlie was not dumb enough to do what the bully told him, but he *was* dumb enough to wrinkle his nose, stick out his tongue, wag his head at him, and perform another rendition of the bumba-latti rap.

The big sixth-grader started throwing himself against the door harder than ever. He was actually trying to break it open! Charlie thought he was living out the story of the big bad wolf blowing down the little pig's house. Terrified, he ran to the phone and dialed the five digit station number. Chris answered the phone and Charlie rattled off what was happening. Chris told him to tell the boy the police were coming and then to get away from the door and hide.

Squire Charlie went to the door, looked at the ogre through the glass pane and said, "My mom called the cops, an' they're friends of ours, an' really big an' mean too, an' they'll be here in a minute, an' they're gonna take you to jail."

Then he ran and hid in Chris's wardrobe. The bully finally left when he heard the sirens wailing. When the police got there, Charlie told them about the bully chasing him and trying to break into the house. They wrote it all down and left. When Chris got home minutes later, Charlie told her everything, except the part where he called the big boy "Fatso" and did the bumba-latty rap.

Chris was soon in touch with the school principal about the sixth-grade bully, and he never bothered Charlie and Alice again. Still, except for Alice, that whole school year was miserable for Charlie, and for Gene too, and their report cards showed it. Charlie should have learned not to say ugly things about how a person looks, but it took a little longer for that lesson to sink in.

That same fall semester, Gene had his own run-in with a kid at school; a skinny beanpole named "Malon," like "May-lun." He was Charlie's age but almost-a-head taller than Gene and really thin. Everybody called him "Skinny Malonie." He liked to attract attention by acting like a big shot. Gene was kind of quiet and didn't make much of a fuss over anything, unlike Charlie, who was always getting into trouble for talking when he should have kept quiet.

One day Gene was walking home after school. When he got to the corner, Skinny Malonie was there waiting for him. Skinny started picking on Gene, just trying to scare him. When he wouldn't let Gene pass, Gene just stepped back, balled up his fist and popped ole' Skinny right in the nose. Skinny's nose started bleeding, and he ran away crying. Gene just went on home. It was a much better and shorter encounter with a schoolyard bully than the one Charlie had. Skinny Malonie acted real nice to Gene after that.

Both Gene and Charlie learned quickly at John B. Cary Elementary that they had to be ever on the alert and ready to fight. If they didn't, they would be picked on and bullied by the likes of the schoolyard ogre and Skinny Malonie. Both of Chris's boys soon got a reputation for being tough kids, though they really hated having to act that way.

CHAPTER 23

OUTLAWS IN TOWN

A side from problems at school, other things were happening on Idlewood Avenue, things that made living there more and more unpleasant. When Chris had proven herself at Mahle's service station, she was trusted to take the money box holding the day's cash receipts home with her at closing time. The money box looked like a steel shoebox with a lock. The habit of taking the box home every night started after burglars broke into the station and stole the cash stash left there for use the next morning.

One night, Chris, Gene and Charlie arrived at home, and Chris got out of the car with the money box in hand. That's when they spotted a strange man standing on the corner under a streetlight no more than 100 feet away. They knew he didn't live close by. The man stood there across the street looking at Chris as she locked her car door and started down the sidewalk with her boys on either side heading toward the house.

As she walked away from the stranger, Chris, in a calm, quiet voice, said, "Boys, don't talk, just keep walking, and don't look back at that man."

The man continued to stand there and watch until they got into the house. He now knew where Chris lived, and Chris knew that he knew.

Not long after that, Chris woke from a dead sleep around midnight to find a man outside, opening her bedroom window. She let out a scream and jumped out of bed, waking Gene and Charlie. The man ran off, and Chris called the police. They came, took a report and looked around outside. Finding nothing, they left. A lot of good that did. Chris figured that in reality, the police were not going to do anything except investigate after a crime was committed, and then try to find who did it.

Whether that prowler was the same man who watched them from the street corner a few nights earlier she never knew, but that did not matter. Between the unwholesome kids at school, the man staring from across the street that night, the prowler and the police's impotence, Chris had had enough. It was time to make some changes that would make her and her boys safe. She did what any smart, young, pretty divorcee with two small kids would do. She got a gun.

Well yeah, a g-u-n! She talked to Sergeant Samuels of the Henrico County Police. He patrolled Lakeside and was a regular at the station. He made arrangements for a confiscated pistol that was slated to be destroyed to instead be legally transferred to Chris, free of cost. She got a concealed carry permit, and that was that.

The gun was a .32 caliber, five-shot revolver, and she carried it loaded to and from work, and whenever she was in the Idlewood neighborhood after dark. That means she was packing heat every night. When she got out of her car, the pistol was in the waistband of her uniform. When she went to bed, it was on her nightstand. It was comforting to her to know she could protect herself and her two children, and she slept a lot better knowing it was there.

Gene and Charlie felt safer too. Chris showed them how the hammer, trigger and safety were used, and sternly lectured them never to pick it up, never play with it, and never even show it to anybody. The boys solemnly promised never to do that. The next day they were telling their classmates about it. Some even came to the house to see it and hold it.

Even at that age the boys understood that a gun was deadly, and they n-e-v-e-r put their finger on the trigger, and never-ever pointed it at a playmate and said, "Bang! Bang! You're dead!" Well, maybe just a couple of times, but they always emptied the cylinder first. Sometimes they imagined all kinds of pretend situations where a burglar or a street bully tried to get into their house while Chris was at the station, or some Indians were chasing a stage coach. They would shoot the bad guys with Chris's gun and save the day. Well, they never really shot the gun. They just pointed the weapon and said, "Bang! Bang! You're dead!"

CHAPTER 24
COMPASSION'S CHILD

C hris was visiting friends who lived close to Idlewood but in Cary Town. It was 1948. A woman's loud screams suddenly shattered the pleasant social chit-chat. Moments later, the woman, a next door neighbor, was banging on the door and hysterically shouting, "Oh, God, help me! Please help me! My husband just cut his wrist. He's killing himself!"

Chris and her friends rushed to the door. Her friends took the woman inside and called the police. Chris ran to the neighbor's house to find her husband. From the entry door she could see into the kitchen. There he was, sitting at the kitchen table, drunk, his chair turned 90 degrees toward the kitchen door. His right elbow rested on the table, with his forearm extended outward in front of him.

Blood poured from his deeply slashed wrist and down to a growing pool between his feet. He sat there, looking back at her. She noted that he was calm, even indifferent to her presence. In his other hand he held a long, bloody butcher knife. His grip on the knife was loose and his wrist relaxed. She went inside and walked toward him. "Hi, my name is Chris. What's yours?" she asked in a casual tone.

"Stony," he answered, politely. He seemed intrigued that she was so calm and unafraid. Chris pulled up a chair and sat in front of him then started talking to the suicidal drunk stranger. She spoke in a friendly, non-judgmental voice. In about two minutes Chris had gotten him to put down the knife and persuaded him to let her dress the wound. She applied a pressure compress made of clean, dry washcloths under a tea towel wrap to soak up any leaking blood. With the bleeding stopped, Chris stayed with Stony, talking to him, getting his mind off his troubles. When he put his face in his hands and began to cry, Chris quietly picked up the knife and moved it out of sight.

Listening to Stony and waiting for the police and ambulance, she learned that he was a WWII vet, had lost most of his friends, and got suicidal when he drank. When Stony heard the sounds of sirens, he started to get agitated and looked over to where he had laid the knife. Chris put her hand on top of his and said sympathetically, "You don't need the knife. No one is going to hurt you, and you don't really want to hurt yourself."

At that moment the police and ambulance arrived out front. Chris continued talking to the distraught man, "They just want to talk to you and patch up your wrist. I'm going out to bring them in now, OK? You just need to sit right here. It'll only take a second. Will you be OK staying here while I go get them?"

Stony's weary, watery eyes looked into hers, then he stoically nodded his assurances. Chris quickly went outside, taking the knife with her. She intercepted the policeman and medics as they stepped onto the porch, quietly explained that the man was in the kitchen was calm, and that she had stopped the bleeding. She urged them to go in quietly and try not to agitate him. She then led them into the house and introduced each of them by name. Stony was still sitting exactly where Chris had left him. As the medic took over and got Stony's attention, Chris slipped the knife to the policeman, and went about wiping up the blood on the floor, table and chair.

Stony lived. He believed his place was with his dead buddies. He received psychiatric care at McGuire Veteran's Hospital. Some months later, after he had completed his therapy, the man and his wife came to see Chris to thank her for saving his life. He said that if she had not cared enough to come to his side and to listen to him, he would have finished the job that night.

CHAPTER 25
FURLOUGHS FROM IDLEWOOD

Chris knew that Idlewood Avenue was not a place for her boys to be unsupervised while she was at work. She looked diligently for opportunities to get them out of there in the summer and into a more fun and healthy place.

On Granny's Farm
When Chris took Gene and Charlie to stay with their Granny it was mostly for a weekend or a week at a time. It was the perfect arrangement, allowing Chris to get her boys out of the city, and a reprieve for Chris.

A single, mature tree dominated the front yard of the farm house. Charlie loved to play in the shade under its full canopy and to it climb it. On one of his excursions up into its many limbs and branches, he fell from halfway to the top. By the grace of God, his fall was stopped short when he landed straddling a strong limb about ten feet off the ground. It was unclear to Charlie what was worse, landing on the ground or the limb. There on Granny's farm Gene and Charlie had many happy days of fun and adventure, even including the farm chores.

One warm, summery night after Granny Morris sent the boys upstairs to bed, Gene whispered to Charlie, "I need to go to the bathroom."

Charlie whispered, "Me too, but I don't wanna use the chamber pot, 'cause I'll just have to empty it and rinse it out in the mornin'."

Gene whispered, "Me neither, but you know that bush Granny planted today?"

Charlie whispered back, "Uh huh."

"Well, Granny said when you plant somethin' you should always give it a good waterin', right?" Gene continued.

"Uh huh," Charlie answered again.

"Well, the bush is right under the window." Gene said, pointing toward the open sash.

Charlie answered enthusiastically, "Yeah! Let's water the bush!"

The two of them climbed out of the bed, went to the window and leaned out. Sure enough, they could see the newly planted shrub directly below, lit up by light from the parlor window.

Ruth, following her nightly habit, was sitting in her rocker in the parlor rocking and reading the newspaper in the peace and quiet at the end of a long day. She paused her reading, looked up, cocked her head and listened intently. She was sure she heard something. She turned to the page with the weather forecast. "Clear overnight, low humidity, mild temperatures."

Her curiosity aroused, she picked up her oil lamp and went to the open window. Holding the lamp beside her head, she bent over and peered out into the darkness. There, not more than three feet from the end of her nose, she beheld two streams of water cascading past her window and into her newly-planted shrub.

Gene and Charlie knew their bedroom window was directly above the parlor window. They knew Granny Morris's rocker was next to the parlor window. They knew she sat in her rocker and read the paper every night. And they knew both windows were open . . . but they didn't connect the dots. Just as Gene and Charlie were happily finishing their watering, the bedroom door swung open. There in the doorway stood Granny, her feet apart, eyes glaring red fire, smoke billowing up like Indian smoke signals from her hair, steam shooting out of both ears, a small tree trunk firmly in her clutches, or so it seemed to the two hapless tadpoles.

The boys, still standing at the window, were frozen in place, eyes wide, mouths agape. They waddled as fast as they could while pulling their underpants up. They jumped in and pulled the sheet and quilt up to their chins. Granny walked over and yanked their protective covering down to the foot of the bed. What happened next was how Gene and Charlie found out where Chris learned to give a whippin. The lesson learned by Gene and Charlie that night lasted, but any harm to the bush was fleeting. Ruth of course told Chris of the incident and her switching the boys' legs with a forsythia frond, and they shared a good laugh.

Aunt Agnes and Uncle Carl

Interspersed with visits to her mother's farm, Chris found other rural places to send her boys. One was a boarding farm out in Chesterfield County. The ad described a spacious three-story house, lots of open play area, fruit growing on the property, a pond for swimming, a swing set and monkey bars, and staff like your children's favorite aunt and uncle. The place was owned by Agnes and Carl Kinderholt. It was sort of like daycare, except they stayed nights too. Chris sent the boys, signing them up for a six week stay.

The owners insisted that they be called Aunt Agnes and Uncle Carl. Agnes seemed warm and kind enough most of the time, but another side of her lurked behind her round, smiling face that seemed to be always flushed pink. Uncle Carl smiled a lot and seemed kind and friendly, but his smile looked unnatural like he wasn't used to it, and he didn't talk much. He was wiry, chain smoked, didn't shave but about every third day, and smelled like he seldom got in the tub. Chris's boys could see through his pretense and had a bad feeling about him; a feeling that would prove to be truer than they could have imagined.

The Kinderholts had fields and woods alright, but the fields were planted in crops, blueberry bushes and blackberry vines. The "swimming pond" was a muddy creek with a red clay dam creating a muddy pool about 12 by 20 feet. The dozen or so kids who were boarding there were allowed to go to the pool once a week. After the girls had their turn, the boys got. That's because the Kinderholts didn't allow boys and girls to swim together. It was "not proper," even though all the children wore bathing suits.

In reality the children aged six or older worked in the fields like hired help on a farm. For a pint of blackberries without blemish or a bushel of corn, a kid was paid one penny. If they worked really hard, they might make 15 cents a day. If a boy didn't produce enough, he was whipped by Carl. A girl not making quota was spanked by Agnes.

Carl Kinderholt was a mean man. He beat the older boys with a razor strop and sometimes hit them with his fists. Any infraction of rules, even ones that had never been told to the kids, set him off. Whenever Uncle Carl went on a tirade, Aunt Agnes stood by and watched. When it was over she applied first aid to the child and softly cooed loving, sympathetic words.

Once, one of the older girls spilled something while helping Agnes in the kitchen. "You stupid brat," Aunt Agnes screamed. "Look what a mess you've made. I'll teach you. Come here."

Embarrassment all over her face, the girl dutifully went to Aunt Agnes, who was standing next to the kitchen work table.

"Now you just bend over this table," shrieked the older woman.

When the frightened girl hesitated, Aunt Agnes grabbed her by the hair and jammed her head down onto the table with a dull thump. Continuing to hold the girl's head down with one hand, she pulled up the girl's dress, pulled down her panties and viciously flailed the girl's bottom with a long-handled spatula. When the beating was over, the poor girl's behind was an ugly mass of raw-looking, swollen flesh, and all the kids saw it.

One day one of the children sneaked into the pantry to steal a fresh peach from the bushel basket that was supposedly for the kids to enjoy. After taking a bite of one, he put it back in the basket. Maybe it was not yet ripe. When Aunt Agnes started to make a peach pie, she discovered the peach with a bite missing. She and Uncle Carl rounded up the kids who had prominent front teeth and tried to match the tooth impressions in the peach to the teeth of the child.

Satisfied that they had found the one who did it, Uncle Carl accused an eight year old boy. Despite denials screamed in terror, Uncle Carl viciously slapped the child with his open hand on the side of his face, knocking him off the chair and onto the floor. The hapless little boy suffered a bruised and swollen cheek and ear.

It was bad enough to have to watch as the Kinderholts beat other kids, but a day came when Gene was beat. He committed some trivial infraction that seemed to be made up on the spot. Uncle Carl grabbed Gene by his arm, flung him around and, with his fist balled tight he punched Gene hard in the face, leaving a badly bruised, swollen cheek and a black eye swollen shut. Charlie seethed with rage at the man and at his own impotence to do anything to help his big brother.

The next day, the Kinderholts' phone rang. Aunt Agnes answered with her sweet, melodious "Hello," ending in a lilt. She listened to the caller, and continued in her honey-smooth voice, "Well, tomorrow would not be the best day. You know regular visitation is on Sunday . . ."

"Oh, I see, but . . ."

"I understand . . ."

"Yes, well, if it's the only day you can get off work, I guess we'll just have to change our plans."

"And we'll be so happy to see you too. What time will you get here? I want to be sure they are clean and dressed properly and not outside playing with the others."

"That's fine. We'll see you tomorrow morning around 10:30. Gu-by-ie." Again, the sing-song lilt at the end.

As Aunt Agnes hung up the phone, the smile on her face morphed into a scowl. She cast an urgent glance at her husband, and the two of them scurried off to their bedroom and closed the door. Minutes later they came back out and called all the kids together. Quickly, all the children were settled down and silent, with half-curious, half-fearful expressions on their faces.

Aunt Agnes said, "I know all of you know the rules. No one calls home unless Uncle Carl or I give you permission. And any letters you want to send home are to be given to us for mailing. Has any of you snuck in here and used the phone or snuck a letter out without us seeing it?"

The kids all shook their heads and said, "No, Ma'am."

Aunt Agnes and Uncle Carl looked hard at each child, but when they got to Chris's boys they stopped and stared menacingly into their faces. Carl growled at Gene, "Did you do it. Did you sneak in here like a dirty little thief and break the rules?"

"No, Sir," said Gene sheepishly, bewildered that he was asked.

Agnes joined in, "What about you, Charlie? It must be you. You did it, didn't you?" she demanded.

"Oh no Ma'am, I didn't do it," lied seven-year-old Charlie. "I didn't!" He pleaded. His apparent innocence was convincing enough for the Kinderholts. They surveyed the kids' faces again.

Then Faye, age thirteen, the oldest of the children and was never beat, asked, "What's wrong, Aunt Agnes?"

Agnes softened her voice and answered without looking at Faye. "We just got a phone call from one of your mothers who is coming here tomorrow for an unscheduled visit."

"Whose mother?" several children asked, hoping it was theirs.

Her voice dripping with disdain, Aunt Agnes said, "It's Gene and Charlie's mother." She glowered at them and commanded in her menacing voice, "Gene and Charlie, you two will keep your mouths shut about how Gene got that black eye and bruise on his cheek. You will tell your mother that he jumped off the swing and fell, and was hit by the swing seat. Do you understand me?"

They nodded their heads, fear evident on their faces. She turned to the other kids and repeated the command. Carl stood up next to her, glared at all the children and said, "If any one of you disobeys Aunt Agnes, I'll beat the hell out of you!"

He then looked each of the other children in the eye and extracted their promise to go along with the story. All the kids lived in dread of Uncle Carl and fearfully promised to obey. They were instructed to tell Chris that they had lots of playtime, and were all having fun. They were told it had better be convincing, or else.

When Chris arrived the next day, Aunt Agnes smoothly laid out her story about how Gene got his bruised cheek and black eye. Then she turned and, with a warm smile and lilting voice, asked the kids, "Isn't that right, children?"

A few of them said yes. Others said nothing. A seemingly long silence followed. Chris was ready to accept the explanation, though her expression showed that she had doubts. Suddenly a boy's voice rang out, "That's not true! That man hit Gene with his fist and said if any of us told on him he would beat us up too!"

Alarm and fear burst onto the faces of all the kids, as they looked to see who had defied the threats. It was Charlie, shouting out through angry tears. Uncle Carl glared at him in stony silence. After a pregnant couple of seconds, Aunt Agnes laughed nervously and said sweetly, "Oh Charlie! Why are you making up a story like that?

Carl Kinderholt looked straight at Charlie. With an ice-cold, malevolent stare, he spit out angrily, "That's a lie! I did no such thing!"

Agnes added, "Charlie, you know your brother fell and hurt himself on the swing. Now tell your mother the truth."

Charlie knew that Carl would, for sure, make good on his warning. He turned to Chris and pleaded with all his heart, "It is too true, Mommy! I saw him do it! He threw our new BB guns out in the cornfield too, an' we had to go find 'em. Oh, Mommy, please don't make us stay. If you leave us he's gonna beat us. He said he would! Please Mommy, take us home now! Please!"

Chris looked at Charlie for a moment, fathoming the subtleties of his expression. Then she looked at Gene, pointed to his bruised cheek and eye and asked calmly, "Son, did that happen like your brother said?"

Gene cut his eyes away and looked down as tears rolled down his cheeks. He slowly nodded his head, "Yes, Ma'am."

Gene looked fearfully at Carl, who glared back at him. Chris surveyed the expressions on all the children's faces and knew that what her sons had said was true. She took her boys home that day.

Soon, she reported the Kinderholts to the state agency that is supposed to be responsible for licensing places like that. Background investigations and oversight of home-based child care like the Kinderholts' was cursory at best. Carl and Agnes Kinderholt eventually lost their license. Whether they went to jail is unknown. From that terrible experience, Gene and Charlie learned that their mother's discipline, however it might sting for the moment, was an act of tough love, not of vengeance.

Emma and Jake

Soon after the Kinderholt trouble, Chris called on her long-time friends, Emma and Jake Wyatt, and asked if they would have Gene and Charlie spend a couple of weeks with them. They had lived in Lakeside for a number of years and were customers of the filling station, but they had recently moved to a farm in the country. When she explained about the Kinderholts, Emma said she would take Gene and Charlie for awhile. That stay was shorter, as it turned out, than even the Kinderholt place.

Both Emma and Jake were hard-bitten people. Jake was brawny, overweight, balding, but had thick hair covering his arms, chest, back and shoulders. His favorite things to do were hunting raccoons for their pelts, drinking bourbon straight up and cussing about politics, government and anything else that didn't suit him. Emma was short, of slight build, had a shrill voice, was crass and cross most of the time and carried a switch, which she used frequently on her children.

The Wyatts, had one daughter, Sally-Jean, their oldest. They also had three sons, two being older than Charlie and one being older than Gene. Sally-Jean sometimes babysat Chris's boys. She let them eat whatever they wanted, and she didn't make them take a nap. She talked to them, read stories to them and played fun games with them. They were always happy when they found out Sally-Jean was coming to babysit them.

The Wyatt boys were another matter. They were earthy to say the least. The two oldest, Bubba and Eddie, got into fist-fights just about every day, and the middle boy teased and tormented the youngest one, Jimmy-Earl, until he turned violent, then beat him up in the name of self-defense. The two older Wyatt boys' idea of fun was to tease Gene and Charlie with lewd, obscene remarks about their pretty mother. Gene, though deeply offended, kept his peace, because he and Charlie were house guests. Besides, he believed the old "sticks and stones" saying.

Charlie was a bit different. He always had trouble holding his tongue at any offense. He was deeply hurt for his mom and felt that Gene and he were being intentionally embarrassed and humiliated. Still, he endured the Wyatt boys' remarks in hopes they would soon tire of it. They did not.

On the morning of their fourth day at the Wyatt's, all the boys were sent to the barn to pull rusty nails out of a pile of salvaged wood planks. The Wyatt boys started right in with their taunting and went on without letup. Charlie couldn't stand it any more. He told them to stop talking about his mother that way. The Wyatt boys just laughed and started teasing him.

Charlie left them working on their chores and went back to the house. He quietly slipped through the screen door and sat in the kitchen where Emma Wyatt was ironing clothes and talking with a neighbor woman. There he seethed and waited to be noticed. Mrs. Wyatt finally spotted Charlie, interrupted her conversation and turned to face him, plainly irritated, her tone cross, "What are you doing sitting in here in the kitchen with us women, boy? Why aren't you out at the barn with the others, helping with the chores?"

Charlie started to cry despite trying very hard not to.

"What're you, a crybaby or somethin'? What're you tuning up about, boy? Answer me!" she screeched.

Charlie mustered his courage and said, "Bubba and Eddie are sayin' nasty things about my mom and won't stop, and it's not nice."

Emma Wyatt exploded. "Why you sniveling little sissy, I'm not gonna have a crybaby in my house. Nosir! I'm gonna send you and that lazy brother of yours right back to your mother."

With that, she picked up the phone and called Chris at the station. When Chris answered, Emma angrily lit into her. "Chris, this is Emma. You need to come and pick up your boys. I want them out of here today. I will not have little sissy boys in my house. I've got enough problems with my own hellions."

Chris knew that any attempt to find out more or to calm Emma down would be futile. "Alright, Emma, I'll leave now and pick them up as soon as I can get there. I'm sorry for whatever brought this on."

When Chris arrived at the Wyatt's farm, Gene and Charlie were already waiting in the yard outside the kitchen door. Their meager clothes and other belongings were loaded into paper grocery bags. They put the bags into the car while Chris headed for the door to the house. Emma saw her coming and came outside, still fuming.There were nothing but harsh words from her, leaving no chance for Chris to ask questions or say anything. Chris, totally surprised at Emma's venom, listened to the rant, saying nothing. When Emma had finished, Chris calmly said she understood, appreciated her keeping Gene and Charlie for her for the several days, then got into the car with her boys and left.

On the way home, she asked the two what had happened. As they described what went on, anger lines appeared on Chris's face and etched ever deeper as she listened. She had known Emma Wyatt as far back as Church Hill. Chris wasn't mad at her boys, but at the fact that Emma, whom she thought was a friend, would tolerate and even blame Chris's boys for the way her own kids had talked and acted.

Once back at the station, her boys with her, Chris called Emma and had a few polite but firm things to say. The short discussion ended with Chris saying she would send them a statement for what they owed the station, after deducting for the cost of Gene's and Charlie's food, and that she expected the Wyatts to pay the balance in full by return mail.

She ended up having to take them to court, but she got what was owed to the staation. Needless to say, Chris and the Wyatt family were no longer friends. Gene and Charlie spent what was left of that summer at home, and in no wise missed the Wyatt's.

On the Reservation

The next summer, 1947, Chris sent her boys to Camp Orapax, a YMCA camp in New Kent County. Most kids stayed for a week or two at most. Gene, Charlie and a handful of other kids stayed for eight straight weeks. Charlie turned eight and Gene was nine-and-a-half. The camp had a Native American theme to it. "Orapax" was an Indian word. The kids were divided into "tribes" by age group: Cherokee, Seminole and Blackfoot. Charlie was Cherokee, Gene a Seminole. That summer, Gene learned to swim.

In February, 1948, for the spring semester, Chris enrolled Gene and Charlie in Lakeside Elementary School in Henrico County.

Though they still lived on Idlwood Avenue in the city, Chris drove them to school before going to work. When school let out in the afternoon, they went to the station and hung out. At closing time the three of them went back to the old rental house in the city, or they went to stay with an afternoon sitter near the school.

The following summer Chris sent them to Camp Orapax for another eight-week stay. That was when Charlie learned to swim. He was so glad to be able to swim like his brother. Camp Orapax was safe, mostly great fun for Gene and Charlie, well supervised, with lots of activities, a large swimming and boating lake, hikes, crafts, campfires at night and chapel every Sunday in an outdoor church in the woods. Some of the older kids called it "the Church in the Wildwood" after the old hymn of similar name.

Chris visited her boys there once in awhile, and the boys had to write postcards to her at least once a week: *"Hi Mommy. I'm having a good time. Today, I caught a salamander in the creek, and a frog too! All the other boys have money to buy things. Can you send me some too, maybe a dollar? Love . . ."*

Chris rarely wrote back, but she did send them a dollar each on one occasion. Other times, Chris sent her boys to stay with their Granny Morris at her farm on Sadler Road. Those days on Granny's farm were by far the best summers Gene and Charlie remembered.

CHAPTER 26
A FUZZY FAREWELL

By September of 1949, Chris was making enough to buy a house in Lakeside and move away from Idlewood Avenue and that declining neighborhood. Moving day morning was overcast, with an unusually mild temperature. Chris and some friends with a panel van truck carried furniture and boxes out the door and onto a truck. Gene and Charlie carried what they could and helped with the cleanup when the house was empty.

After what seemed like several hours, the job was done. Chris, the last one out, locked the front door. She took extra care to lock both the latch and the heavy-duty dead bolt. It was time to leave.

The truck engine roared to life and in a moment pulled away from the curb. Gene and Chris got into their mom's black Pontiac, ready to overtake the truck and be at the new house when it arrived. Charlie headed toward the car. One last toy dangled from his hand – "Fuzzy," his teddy bear. Charlie stopped and took one long, last look at the house and savored the joy of leaving it and that unhappy place forever.

Chris called out through the open car door, her mood cheerful, "Charlie, come on, get in the car. It's time to go."

Gene added, "Come on, Squirt. Get in the car!"

The teddy bear had been Charlie's best friend in the whole world. Fuzzy had comforted him, eased his fears, absorbed his tears and hugged him to sleep every night during the last, dying months of his mom and dad's marriage and for many months after they separated. Charlie looked for a long moment at Fuzzy, with his split seam, missing button and stitched smile. He then drew back his arm and hurled Fuzzy up onto the porch roof. "Bye, Fuzzy!" he called out, then turned and with a beaming smile ran to the car, jumped in and closed the door.

Chris glanced at Charlie as she drove off. "Why did you throw Fuzzy up on the roof like that?" she asked, her tone mildly disapproving.

"Cause he's all worn out. And besides, I'm too old for a teddy bear now." He knew that Fuzzy belonged with that house and that street, and all the troubles that Fuzzy had helped him through. He belonged in the past. As the car pulled away and headed toward Lakeside and a new life, a faint smile crept across Chris's face. Her youngest was no longer a little boy.

Chris arrived at 2302 Kent Street, her very own home, titled in her name alone. She and her boys were greeted by the real estate agent, Mr. Hoffman. He presented Chris and the boys with a house-warming gift – a kitten, black male with a white star on his chest and white boots. Chris named him "Mr. Hoffman." The kitten moved in with Chris and her boys from day one. In the fullness of time, Mr. Hoffman became monarch of Kent street and succeeded in training his three staff humans to meet his every wish and command.

The house in Lakeside was a modest bungalow, built by its former owner. It was a little smaller than most of the surrounding houses, but it had a big, detached two car garage, two trees in the front yard and a big back yard. A four foot high fence made of cedar posts and hog wire ran along the back property line. Sitting in the corner of the back yard was a tall tree. To Charlie, it seemed to say, *Hey you. Come climb me if you dare.*

The neighbor behind the house was a chicken farmer. He had a long, one-story chicken coop running parallel to the fence and sitting just a few feet inside his property. Beyond that was his house, which faced the next street over, Nelson Street. Beside the farmer's house and chicken coop was an open field a quarter of a block square. The kids living on Kent and Nelson soon claimed it as their exclusive playground.

At that time, Chris's house was one of only four in the 2300 block of Kent Street. The rest of the block was vacant lots. That is where Gene and Charlie grew up, and where they have many memories, mostly warm ones, including memories of Gene playing with the Chemistry set he got for Christmas and Charlie climbing that tree in the back yard.

He would climb as high up in it as the limbs and branches would carry him. Even on a windy day, when the treetop swayed under wind gusts and tried to shake him loose, Charlie would be up there, holding fast and thrilled with excitement.

The move to Lakeside was life-changing for Chris and her boys. There were no strangers hanging out on street corners watching her when she came home after dark. Her boys did not have to face schoolyard bullies, at least as long as they were in elementary school, and the other kids in their classes were all decent and wholesome. The main downside to living in Lakeside was that Gene and Charlie were the only kids in their classes whose parents were divorced. They were keenly aware of that fact and of the stigma attached to it.

They both made friends and soon fit right in. They were happy, and Charlie was particularly relieved and grateful for escaping John B. Carry School, even if it meant giving up Princess Alice. Chris was able to get to and from work in less than five minutes. That meant she could keep better control of her boys, and it was a far safer place. They were among people like themselves, folks working to support a family and a better future. It was a watershed event in lives of Chris and her boys.

Charlie remembers no more whippings after the move to Lakeside. Gene thinks he might have had one more. Either way, the early lessons taught by Chris's belt stuck. The boys were happier, and they behaved themselves better . . . well, at least a little better. They were not the "Leave it to Beaver," nor the "Ozzie and Harriet" boys, and they didn't sing in any church choir, but they improved.

Chris still had her gun, but she didn't have to carry it to and from work. It mainly stayed in the drawer of her nightstand except when Gene or Charlie took it out to play with it and show off to their new friends.

CHAPTER 27

THE NEED FOR SPEED

The first brand new car Chris bought was a 1948 Nash Ambassador, two door coupe, with a straight-8 engine. The car had the ability to go fast, which Chris used often. It also sported a spotlight mounted on the driver-side corner post. It was a popular extra that sometimes came in handy, like when she was trying to read a street sign or a house number in the dark, or when a headlight had burned out.

On one occasion she took Gene and Charlie, and one of her female buddies and her buddy's kid for a day trip to "th' rivah." In Richmond, that usually meant the Rappahannock River. The route was mostly a two-lane, secondary road. Chris's boys could see the speedometer start to climb when they came to straight and level stretches. She topped it out at 90 before slowing again for the next curve.

Some people might think that was just a tad reckless, even for a modern interstate highway, and they'd be right. But during the years following World War II, people were looking for the excitement and maybe a bit of the thrill of danger – the elevated adrenalin they had felt during the war years. Fast cars and motorcycles were favorite ways of getting that rush. Besides, Chris was a single woman in her 20s and was doing pretty well.

She could be forgiven if she was a little full of herself. Let him or she who has never felt the-need-for-speed cast the first stone.

One evening after closing the station, Chris and her boys got in the Nash and headed out, with Gene and Charlie in the back seat. It was a hot night and the windows were rolled down. For some reason, she decided to go home by way of Dumbarton Road to Staples Mill, then to Dickens Road and on to Broad Street. At that time, Dickens was paved only with rolled gravel. As she approached Dickens, she noticed a Henrico County policeman on a motorcycle. Henrico Police had very few officers at that time, and Chris was on a first-name basis with all of the ones who patrolled the Lakeside-Greendale area. The motorcycle cop appeared to be her friendly customer, Patrolman Dave Richardson.

On playful impulse, Chris gunned the gas, spun tires on Staples Mill asphalt and through the turn onto Dickens and took off. As she fully expected, the motorcycle gave chase. Chris ignored the siren for maybe a half-mile, weaving and kicking up a cloud of dust and gravel before she finally pulled over and stopped.

She waited with a smile for Dave to come up to her window, where she was sure he would join her in a good laugh. When the patrolman took off his goggles, he looked like a raccoon, which made it impossible to take him seriously, though he desperately wanted her to. Surprise, surprise, the officer was not Dave Richardson. He was instead a young, very green recruit with a name tag saying he was Art Goodman. He did not know her from Adam, or rather, Eve, and she for sure had never seen him before. Anger was written all over Officer Goodman's dust-covered face.

Trying hard to stifle her laughter and put on a serious expression, Chris apologized profusely, and explained that she thought he was Dave Richardson, a long-time friend and customer of the station. The rooky officer calmed down, excused himself, went back to his bike, and wiped his face as clean as he could with a rag retrieved from his saddle bag.

When he came back to the car window, he said he had thought it over and decided to let her go. With a half-serious warning, a genuine smile and an appreciative glance at Chris, he said he might drop in at the station sometime, if that was alright with her. She thanked him, said that would be fine and she would be looking for him.

That's when it became clear to Chris that times were changing, that Henrico County PD was expanding as fast as the county's population, and she could no longer assume she would know every officer she might run into. Officer Goodman did stop by the station, but nothing developed between Chris and him.

One dark Friday in the fall of 1949 in the evening hours, Chris, still in her work uniform, was driving Gene and Charlie to Granny Morris's farm for the weekend. She was on Broad Street Road headed west, several miles from any built-up area. She saw a set of fresh, parallel skid marks on the pavement, veering to the left, then right. The distance between them spreading apart before going over the shoulder.

A few cars were parked along both sides of the road, some with their headlights still blazing. A small crowd of people were leaving their cars and gathering on the right shoulder. Several of them pointed down into the ditch as they talked to each other. There, in the darkness at the bottom of the seven foot deep ditch was a car lying upside down, smoke and water vapor slowly drifting up from the wreckage and becoming visible in the headlights at street level. From the skid marks and the people still gathering, it looked like the overturned car had been speeding way too fast, had gone into a skid and done a 180-degree spin before rolling into the ditch just moments before.

Chris pulled to the side of the road and stopped. She turned on her car's spotlight and trained it on the wreckage. "You boys stay in the car 'til I get back. I'll only be a couple of minutes," she commanded, her tone dead serious.

She scrambled out, shut the door with a firm thump, and ran to the crash. From the top of the bank, she could see two legs with pants and shoes protruding from under the overturned car. No one was doing anything except gawking and talking. Gene and Charlie rolled the car window down so they could hear and see.

Chris looked at the dozen or so bystanders and asked in a loud voice, "Is he alive?"

A woman spoke up and said, "We don't know. Nobody's been down there to find out.'

"He's dead for sure." a man chimed in.

"Has an ambulance been called?" Chris asked.

Another voice in the crowd said, "Somebody left a couple of minutes ago. I thought they were going to find a phone."

Chris looked at the bystanders, frowned, and with three short hops was at the bottom of the ditch. She dropped to her knees and tried to look under the car. "Hello! Can you hear me?" she asked. A moment passed. Suddenly, she turned and yelled up to the crowd, "He's alive! I can hear him! Some of you men come roll this car off so we can pull him out."

Several men jumped into the ditch, put their backs and shoulders into it and rolled the car up enough to take the pressure off the trapped man. While they held the car, Chris and one of the men pulled the semi-conscious man from under the still-smoldering wreckage. Chris and three men quickly carried the man up the embankment and laid him on an overcoat that someone had taken off and spread for him.

Chris checked him over. He was cut and bruised, but the bleeding was not profuse. His chest looked unnaturally flat. Urgency and authority evident in her tone, Chris said, "He's got to get to Medical College Hospital. He can't wait for an ambulance. Can anybody here take him?"

The silence was shameful. Finally, one voice said, "I don't want to get blood all over my seat covers."

Chris didn't have time to reply to that. Hearing nothing more, she commanded, "Help me put him in the back seat of my car. I'll take him. I need someone to look after my two sons 'til I get back."

A lady spoke up: "My husband and I will stay right here with them. They'll be safe." The lady's husband gave her a questioning looked. She glared back at him as she shouted to Chris, "You take as long as you need, Miss. You're a brave woman- braver than most any of us."

Two other couples joined in. "We'll stay too."

"Thanks," said Chris, and beckoned to Gene and Charlie to get out of the car. She turned again to the crowd. "One of you go find the nearest phone and call the police. Tell them I'm coming down Broad Street, heading for MCV. Tell them the situation and that I'm driving that Nash over there. I'll be flashing my high beams and my spotlight will be on."

Gene, now almost 12 and Charlie, 10, got out of the car and waited by the roadside while Chris and two men put the badly-injured man on the back seat. She then jumped in, fired it up, did a U-turn, and headed east down Broad Street Road as fast as she dared go, headlights flashing between high and low, spotlight blazing, and horn honking at other cars that got in the way. She was soon met by a police car that apparently had gotten the message. With emergency lights flashing and siren wailing He escorted Chris the rest of the way down Broad Street to the MCV emergency room.

As it turned out, several couples stayed with her boys. After two hours or more, Chris returned. She rolled to a stop where her boys and some adults were standing. She explained to the one remaining couple that the police had her stay at the hospital until they could collect information on the injured man and take her statement.

The man's chest had been crushed, and he had internal, bleeding injuries. The doctors at the ER told Chris and the policemen that he was still alive, that she had gotten him there in the nick of time, and that he was critical but might live.

Chris, Gene and Charlie then went on to Ruth's farm on Sadler Road. It was after eleven when they arrived. Ruth was worried and asked what had taken so long. Chris, Gene and Charlie told Ruth the whole story as they ate a plate of cold fried chicken, mashed potatoes, string beans, a biscuit and a glass of sweet tea.

Chris never found out if the stranger in the ditch lived, but she was at peace with the knowledge that she had done all she could to save him. Gene and Charlie were a little anxious, cold and hungry standing on the side of the dark, country road with strangers, but they were none the worse for the experience. They were also awed by what their mother had done and were as proud of her as they could be. From Gene and Charlie's own lips the word quickly spread around Lakeside about Chris's heroic action, and the story spread from one school kid to the next, and from kids to parents.

CHAPTER 28
GRANNY'S DRIVEWAY

On Ruth Morris's Sadler Road farm, she had turkeys, chickens, a goat named Nanny and a massive brood sow named Sook Pig, (sounds like "book"). She was black all over and weighed at least 500 pounds. She resembled a large whiskey barrel turned on its side, with four squatty peg legs and a huge head with floppy ears, each the size of a leaf of collard greens, and a corkscrew tail.

Sook produced a lot of healthy piglets. In exchange for this service, she was given privileged treatment. Though Sook could not speak English and Ruth could not speak Pig-lish, they both understood their symbiotic relationship and seemed to know what the other wanted and expected.

Ruth often fetched old Sook from the pigpen at the edge of the woods about 40 yards behind the house, and the two of them would go for a walk down that long driveway through the wheat field. Along the way, the old sow always stopped and scratched her side against the bumper of Ruth's 1934 Chevy coupe – the one with the rumble seat that Gene and Charlie loved to ride in. Sook would scratch so hard that she'd set the car to rocking as if it the two were dancing. Why, sometimes it looked like the old Chevy might flip over on its side, but it never did.

When Sook's itch was satisfied she and Ruth would set out like two old friends on a leisurely stroll down the driveway. It had to be leisurely, because old Sook only had two speeds, slow and lie down. The driveway ran right through the middle of that wheat field. The driveway was so full of ruts and potholes that a car could not drive down it at more than about five miles an hour.

They'd stroll the whole quarter-mile to pick up the mail and evening newspaper, and then stroll back. Sook had to stop two or three times along the way to cool off in a muddy pothole. When Ruth was ready to resume their walk, Sook somehow knew and would pick herself up and set out again. They'd walk together out and back, ending at the pigpen where Sook waited like a lady for Ruth to open the gate and let her in.

Usually at the beginning and end of a walk Ruth would scratch Sook behind her ears. The old sow seemed to know Ruth's scratching was a show of fondness. Sook gave her an appreciative grunt whenever she did it.

One hot mid-summer evening, after taking Sook to get the mail, Ruth, Gene, Charlie and Perk, who was visiting but not living there, were sitting on the front porch waiting for Chris to come from work. Ruth and the boys had been shelling butter beans and snapping snap beans for some time. They were all expecting Chris to turn into the driveway at any time.

As they made small talk and watched for Chris in the fading summer twilight, crickets began to chirp, frogs did their "ree-deep" thing, and lightning bugs came out by the thousands, flashing their lanterns over the yard and wheat fields. A whippoorwill could be heard off in the distance sending its lonesome call rippling through the calm air. The night ski, free of urban light pollution, glittered with millions of white diamonds coalesced into a wide strand that spanned from horizon to horizon, the Milky Way.

Finally, a pair of headlights appeared off in the distance coming down Sadler Road. Moments later the lights turned onto

Granny's driveway. Ruth, Perk and they boys knew it had to be Chris. Curiously though, just after turning into the driveway, the headlights stopped moving.

Moments later, a third light appeared. Unlike the bright, steady beams of the headlights, it was yellow and seemed to be blinking. All eyes on the porch were straining to figure out why the head-lights were not moving. Then they heard a faint noise, possibly a voice. Perk jumped to his feet. Urgently he barked, "It's Chris! She's calling for help! Her car is on fire!"

At six foot four, long-legged, and no more than his mid-twen-ties old, Perk bounded off that porch and down the driveway like an Olympic sprinter. Gene and Charlie took off behind him just as fast as they could.

Ruth called out after them, "You boys come back here. Don't you go out there, ya hear! You stay here with me! That car might blow up!"

The boys pretended not to hear her and kept right on running.

Perk got to the car first and found the hood open, tongues of fire leaping up from the engine and black smoke billowing out. Chris was scooping mud from a pothole and throwing it at the fire. Perk quickly joined her, throwing mud fast and furious. By the time Gene and Charlie got there the flames were out, though smoke continued to curl up from the car.

Perk looked Chris over to see if she was alright. Her hair and eyebrows were singed, mud was smeared on her face, hands and arms, and splattered all over her work uniform. She realized Perk and her boys were studiously looking at her. "What?" she said to Perk, somewhat indignantly, as she shrugged and turned her palms up.

She was fine, just fine. Perk and the boys' expressions went from worry to smiles, to snickers, then into full out laughter.

"What?" Chris repeated, more insistently.

"You should see yourself, Sis," Perk said good-naturedly. "You're a mess."

Chris felt her face and hair, looked at her uniform and joined in the laughing as her fear and worry melted away. It turned out that the fire was caused by a gasoline leak ignited by a spark most likely from the generator armature or the points. Chris didn't notice it until she slowed to turn into the driveway. The wind from Chris's need-for-speed had helped suppress the flames while she was on the road.

The paint was burned off the front end of the car, the engine was damaged and everything under the hood that could burn did: wires, rubber hoses, the battery and so on. Perk asked Chris why she hadn't run away from the car for fear of an explosion. Chris said she wanted to save her car more than she feared it blowing up.

The white metal parts, like the carburetor and fuel pump, were melted. The lead-and-copper radiator was also melted, as were all the rubber hoses. The hood and front fenders were buckled, the paint burned to bare metal. In short, the car was ruined between grill and firewall, leaving the passenger compartment, roof, doors, rear fenders and trunk unharmed.

Most people would think the car was a total loss, but then Chris was not like most people. The next day, she called the station and had the service truck come tow the burned-out car back to the shop, where she rebuilt it, with a few "minor" changes.

She "souped it up" with a high performance ignition system, four barrel carburetor, a high-output fuel pump, bored out the cylinders and valve ports, put in a racing cam, and applied undercoating to the frame and sheet metal in the engine compartment to absorb vibration, dampen noise and prevent rust.

When all that was done the Nash was ready for a new paint job from bumper to bumper. Chris collected auto paints left over from other jobs and blended them into what she described as, a "snazzy color." It included a generous helping of sparkling powder made from fish scales that was used to give paint that glittery metallic look.

When the car was rolled out into the sunlight for the first time, it changed color. At night the color changed as it passed through different patches of illumination along the street. In bright sunlight it looked like a sort of metallic, sparkly silver with a greenish highlight that seemed to shimmer along the curves. In the shade, it looked more like a medium green with a hint of pink and silver highlights.

When Chris drove down the street, pedestrians would stop to look at it as she drove by. When it was parked, they would stop, bob up and down, move left or right, stand on their toes, squint, and close one eye then the other, just to watch it change colors. They were simply fascinated by the way the paint changed as their position changed, or as the type, source and direction of light changed.

If you notice things of that sort, you may know that such iridescent, multicolor, metallic paint effects are popular even today on motorcycles and custom cars. Back then, it was unknown . . . until Chris did it. Others may have come up with it too, independently of her, but Chris was, if not the first, certainly one of the first to do it.

Not only was the restored Nash Ambassador an eye-popper, with the tricked out engine the thing was wickedly fast. If she jammed the gas pedal to the floorboard it would lay rubber for sixty feet and pin you to your seat. Chris took the car to a place called "Broadus Flats," where gearheads took their hotrods to see what they could do.

Chris wound that big-block Nash up to top speed. The engine was so powerful that when it hit 125, the exhaust blew the muffler off the car. It blew the muffler . . . clean off, I mean clean off . . . the car! And to think, all it had under the hood was an old-fashioned, flat-head straight-8. Those were generally not in the league of the latest hot, V-8 Ford engines . . . but this one was. It got about 12 miles to a gallon, but who cared – high-test gas was only 22 cents a gallon. Chris turned a pretty powerful family coupe into a beast. That engine should have been in an Air Force fighter plane.

CHAPTER 29
PEACE AND STABILITY

C hris continued to grow in skill and competence. By 1952, the year she turned 33, she had been working at the station for eight years. She was making such a contribution to the business that Dick Mahle made her his business partner, albeit only a 10 percent one. They never bothered to see a lawyer to get something written up and signed. They were partners and trusted each other completely.

Chris moved from an hourly wage to a salary, and her salary was more than she had been making from the long, grueling hours. In fact, it was more than any other employee. When all that was agreed on, Mahle called a short meeting out in the shop for all the employees. After everyone was assembled, he announced that from then on, Chris was boss after him. When ever he was not there, she had full authority. What she says goes, and they were not to come complaining to him about her decisions. They were to obey her as they did him; that if anyone gave her a hard time they would answer to him. It turned out that the speech was anti-climactic. The other employees already liked and respected Chris's mechanical skills, her knowledge, how she treated them and how she handled problems. For Chris, her days in the sun had arrived.

With Chris's income rising, she and her boys ate well, including having steak for dinner regularly. Charlie had to wear fewer hand-me-downs, and Chris eventually bought a TV set, though Gene and Charlie were the last kids in their school classes to have one. The first TV station in Richmond, WTVR, Channel 6, came on the air in April, 1948.

TV sets were in stores and people were buying them. Though most of their classmates had TVs, it was several years before Gene and Charlie saw a "Howdy Doody" show on their own TV, and they both had a crush on the actress who played Princess Summer-Fall-Winter-Spring.

Emmett reentered the lives of Chris and the boys the winter when Charlie was 11 years old and Gene barely 13. He was a sergeant in the National Guard, on active duty with the 3647th Maintenance Depot at Bellwood, off US-1 near the DuPont plant in south Richmond. His drinking was controlled, he had a second wife, Thelma, and he had been faithful in his child support payments. Both Chris and Emmett had settled down and were moving up in their new lives.

Chris graciously allowed him liberal visitation, which proved to be helpful to all concerned. She and Emmett grew mutually respectful and cooperative, though not what you'd call friends. Emmett helped Chris guide their sons through their 'tween and early-to-mid-teen stages. He would sometimes ask for Chris's thoughts on a mechanical problem, which she happily gave him, and she would occasionally call and ask him for help with the boys, to take them for a day or a weekend.

Emmett and Thelma lived on the National Guard base, where repairs were made on everything from pistols to artillery pieces, jeeps to trucks and tanks. On that base, Emmett told Gene and Charlie about "the birds and bees," but it wasn't any more than they had already learned in the boys' bathroom at school. He also taught them to drive. He started them on a Jeep, graduated to trucks, and then to tanks. Now that was some serious fun for Charlie, age 12, and Gene, 13-1/2, and it saved a lot of wear and tear on Chris's car.

The base had a small firing range where Emmett taught the boys to shoot. The lessons started with a Browning 1911, .45 caliber pistol, an M-1 carbine, then graduating to the M-1 rifle, the weapon that General Dwight Eisenhower said was the weapon that won the ground war in World War II. It is hard to think of anything Emmett could teach his sons that was more fun than driving Jeeps, trucks and tanks, and shooting guns.

When Emmett's dog had puppies, he gave the boys the pick of the litter. It was female, had long curly, white hair with black spots floppy ears and a natural bobbed tail. When it was weaned, Gene and Charlie took the puppy home. They were girded for battle over an expected "no way" answer from Chris, but it was love at first sight. She named the pup Stinker.

Mr. Hoffman, the cat, grudgingly allowed Stinker to live. He even trained her. Eventually, Mr. Hoffman would even allow Stinker to sleep next to him – sometimes. It was a treat which Stinker very much enjoyed. Mr. Hoffman terrorized all the free-roaming dogs within a three block radius and impregnated all the female cats.

Stinker, on the other hand, loved everybody and every animal she encountered. The mailman, milkman, paperboy, meter readers, even strangers were greeted by Sinker, wagging all over and licking them like they were her long lost family.

CHAPTER 30
TAKING OVER

In the filling station business, certain major financial events occur regularly. One of them is paying for a 30,000 gallon load of gasoline delivered by the wholesale supplier into the underground tanks.

Every time one of those gas deliveries came, Dick Mahle had to scramble to scrape together the needed money, or go to the bank and borrow enough to meet the payment, which was due upon delivery. He always threw a fit about the cost, the demand for payment on delivery, and his not having the cash in hand to cover it.

Chris thought it was pretty "stoopid," as she pronounced it for emphasis, not to plan for that in advance. She opened a savings account in the station's name and regularly deposited a little of the daily receipts into it. The total gallons sold each day, times the current wholesale price per gallon determined the amount to be set aside for that day.

Mahle actually knew nothing about that until the first large payment came due after Chris had started the savings program. As he went on fussing, cussing and complaining about having to come up with the money to pay for the load of gas, Chris said, "We already have the money, and we didn't need to take out a loan."

He kept on ranting for about a half-sentence, then stopped in the middle of a word and said, "Wha' did you say?"

She repeated herself and added, "I set aside a little everyday and put it in a savings account."

She then showed him the passbook for the account. Mahle was pleased as punch and impressed. He asked, "How in the world did you come up with that idea?"

Chris, with a twinkle in her eye and a smile, answered, "A little birdie told me."

When the time came for him to leave for the day, he proposed a shot of bourbon to celebrate. Naturally, all the employees joined in, Chris included.

From then on, Mahle just left all financial affairs of the business to her, and he took home more money during those years than he had ever made before. He also now had time at the station to play gin rummy with his buddies, guys he knew from Masonry and from Hatcher Memorial Baptist Church.

Chris learned principles of accounting and bookkeeping, and kept the books for the business. Then she took over all the payroll records, tax filings, bill paying and collecting delinquent accounts. All that saved accountant fees and time.

She was in court so often collecting from non-paying customers that Henrico County District Court Judge Dickson Powers and she were on a first name basis, and he let her conduct the cases and get judgments on her own without a lawyer. That was allowed because the station was not an incorporated business but a partnership, and she was a partner. In effect she was representing herself.

In the course of trying to collect unpaid repair bills, Chris learned a trick or two that sometimes got the debt paid without having to go to court. If a customer could not pay his bill but sold products or provided services that the station could use, she would work it out so they paid with those rather than money.

In some instances when she got a judgment against a deadbeat customer but could not collect it in cash, she put a judgment lien on the customer's property. When they found out they couldn't sell or refinance the property, they paid the debt, plus interest, court costs and attorney fees if she used one.

In some cases, if the non-paying customer owned a business, she would bide her time and let the customer think he had beat the station out of the debt. Then she would hire him to do a job for the station, or buy something for the station from him on credit. When the non-payer sent her a bill, she would simply mail it back with a note saying, "Offset against your debt to Dick Mahle Service station."

Sometimes the customer would yell and scream and demand payment, but it made no difference. If they sued for their bill, the judge would agree that Chris had the right by law to offset the two debts. Lawyers and judges call it "the right of setoff and recoupment." Surprise!

Chris continued to drive her snazzy Nash until a customer, who was also a hot-rodder, showed up at the station and asked if he could see it. Chris was happy to show it to him. Next he wanted to take it for a ride. Chris went with him, of course. By the time he got back to the station he just had to have that car.

"Would you consider selling it?" he asked.

Chris replied, "I haven't thought at all about selling it, but if the price is right, I guess I would."

After some discussion, Chris reluctantly let it go, but her pain of parting with it was eased, at least a little, by the wad of cash she made off it. She replaced that car in the fall of 1952 with her very first special-order, ultra feminine and well equipped, spanking new car. It was a 1953 Mercury sport hardtop: sleek, pale metallic blue body wrapped around Merc's most powerful V-8 engine, leather upholstery, a moon-roof, factory tinted glass all around, fender skirts on the rear wheel wells and whitewall tires.

Designed by Chris, it looked, smelled, felt like and oozed a blend of feminine luxury and raw power. When idling, it purred like a lioness lounging in the shade after dining on a fresh gazelle. Chris's new Merc' was a sublime statement, though it never crossed her mind to make one. It *was* Chris.

Chris ruminated a while on that second resale, and thought there could be profit in buying damaged cars, fixing them up and flipping them. There wasn't any real planning and talking about it. She just put the word out to other shops and to the service departments of dealerships.

When an attractive opportunity came along she suggested it to Mahle. He went for it, and it worked out well. He was on board. Next thing you know they were regularly buying, fixing, dressing up and flipping cars. It was a whole new profit center that kept the employees working and earning money when repair business was slack.

CHAPTER 31
NATURE'S BOUNTY

Chris sometimes planted a vegetable garden in her backyard on Kent Street. When she did, she pitched right in, drafted Gene and Charlie for help with the plowing, hoeing, sowing and weeding, all done by hand. She planted a few hills of corn, some tomatoes, cucumbers, peppers, carrots and string beans.

All of her plants came up and bore some produce, though not plentiful. That might have been because of poor soil, heat and draught, or, more likely, from lack of regular watering by Gene and Charlie. They were old enough to have worked that garden to make it produce, but Chris wasn't home to make them do it, and they tended the garden as kids that age typically do — as little as possible.

In the long run it didn't matter much, because Henry got himself a quarter-acre garden patch, which he planted and tended faithfully and which rewarded his TLC with a cornucopia of succulent, good-eating veggies. From his prodigious surplus he supplied Chris with much of the fresh produce she and her boys ate during the growing season.

Chris had better luck growing flowers, which she did mostly at the station, where she could tend them regularly. Since she spent most of her waking hours there, she also got to enjoy them more than if they had been planted at home.

Sometime around 1954, an old Native American Indian, Chief Custalow, became an occasional customer at the station. He was the real chief of a real reservation tribe, the Mattaponi (Mat-ta-po-ni). Their reservation lies along the Pamunkey River. By state law, members of a recognized Virginia tribe could fish and hunt any time of the year without licenses, tags or limits.

The old chief took a shine to Chris and she to him. That was all it took for him to treat her like a daughter. That, it turned out, meant Chris could get striped bass and shad during spawning season. That was because, *Paleface not allowed – go to jail if catch shad or stripe bass in roe time. But OK for Indian. Good eating.*

Sometimes, the chief would just show up at the station and hand her some fresh fish on ice. Other times, he would phone the station, and she would drive down to the reservation and pick them up. Shad roe is a rare delicacy, and, when fried and served with eggs for breakfast, it is delicious. It's a type of American caviar. Chris *knew* how to bake shad – slow, in a covered roast pan with seasoning and veggies, at 200 degrees for about seven hours.

Shad is notorious for having so many small bones it is hardly worth trying to pick them out. But, when cooked that way, the bones dissolve and flavor the meat. Uumm, uum, good!

When Chris's boys were teenagers, they went fishing with their friends pretty regularly. Of course, it was freshwater fishing - much different from salt water. They would catch silver perch, bluegills, large-mouth bass and even an occasional pike. One time Charlie even brought home a mess of bullfrog legs. It didn't matter. Chris was always happy to cook whatever they caught, and when she cooked their catch, it was always tasty.

CHAPTER 32

THE SPIRIT OF CHRISTMAS PAST

C hris was standing behind the counter at the station in mid-December, 1953 when the phone rang. She answered with a smile that put a lilt in her voice. "Dick Mahle Service . . . Oh, hi, Brother, Merry Christmas!"

As Henry Morris talked, the seasonal cheerfulness drained from Chris's face. Moments later she began to cry softly. When the short call ended she broke into sobs. She was sullen and intermittently cried the rest of that day. She told Dick Mahle privately about the call, and he urged her to take the afternoon off. She refused, saying she would rather keep working to take her mind off of it.

Chris was still sullen and grieving that evening when she got home. She called Gene and Charlie to the living room and had them sit down. Her face told them something was seriously wrong. They prepared for bad news. Their mother began to speak but broke into uncontrollable crying before getting out a single word.

Fearing the worst and ready to go knock someone silly for hurting his Mom, Gene asked urgently, "What's wrong, Mom?"

When she tried to continue, Chris could not answer before breaking down again. She left the room and returned more composed several minutes later. She sat down again and began to speak, fighting tears with each short, stabbing phrase.

"Brother called . . . Perk lost his job. He . . ." As her tears began to overflow again, Chris forced out her words between wrenching sobs, "has gone back to Fluvanna . . . to the old farmhouse. Those precious babies in the cold, barefoot . . . all they have . . . little shorts and tee shirts, no winter clothes, no food to get through winter."

At that, she broke down completely. Perk and his family were now reliving that terrible time in 1930, when their parents lost everything and had to go back there and live in the old house that had been boarded up since 1920. Chris's painful memories of that time a generation earlier compounded her agony over Perk's situation. When she finally regained her composure, she continued. "I'm sorry to be crying like this, boys, but the thought of those precious little babies suffering like that just breaks my heart. Can you understand that?"

Gene and Charlie nodded. They could not truly understand their mother's pain, but they could plainly see how deep it was. They felt sorry for Uncle Perk, Aunt Jesse and their cousins, but they were more upset that their mom was in so much misery. The boys assured her that they understood.

"I can't just let them suffer like that and not do something. I just can't. Do you understand?" she asked again.

Gene and Charlie again assured her it was alright, that they understood.

Chris continued, "Would it be alright with you boys if you don't get Christmas presents this year, and if I use that money to buy some winter clothes and food for those babies?" Agony and desperation etched deep lines in her face as she looked first to Gene, then to Charlie. "You know, we don't have enough money to do both. Is that OK with you boys?"

By that time Charlie was in tears himself, but having recently turned 14, he was really trying hard not to show it. Gene was visibly moved but not crying. They reassured their mother several times that it was OK with them. They would do anything to end the emotional suffering of their mother.

Days later, her car loaded with gifts and Charlie riding with her, Chris drove out to that place along the lonely country road in Fluvanna and turned into the old, familiar dirt road flanked by woods and scrub brush. The car bumped along through the ruts and muddy wallows that seemed bigger and definitely worse than Ruth Morris's driveway at her farm house.

They finally broke into a clearing and rolled to a stop near the house. Charlie, who had never seen the place before, looked it over. The wood siding was unpainted, split in places, the gaps covered with cardboard on the inside. The tin roof was rusted through in places. The chimney was cracked and leaning away from the outside wall. A window pane was broken and covered with cardboard. Makeshift steps led up to the door. In the years when it stood empty, vandals and weather had taken their toll.

Chris and Charlie got out of her car and walked toward the house. Perk, towering six foot four, with broad shoulders and thick, reddish-brown, crew-cut hair, answered the door with his big smile. "Hi, Perk," said Chris.

"Hi Sis, Charlie is that you? Look how tall you are! Come on in," he said as he patted Charlie on the shoulder.

Once inside he quickly closed the door. A fire crackled in the fireplace, and the room was surprisingly warm and cozy. The smell of burning wood and the fresh-cut cedar Christmas tree added a pleasant, seasonal aroma to the room.

Jesse came from another room and affectionately greeted them as she took a position at Perk's side. The kids, all much younger than Charlie, quickly gathered around hugging their parents' legs and looking at the visitors.

Jesse, always a warm hostess, said, "What a nice surprise to see you, Chris, and you too Charlie. My, goodness, how you've grown since I saw you last! You all come sit down."

She ushered Chris and Charlie to the sofa that sat in front of the rustic fireplace and seated herself in an overstuffed wingback chair that sat at a 90-degree angle to the sofa. Perk, remained standing next to Jesse's chair. Questions by Jesse followed about Henry and Elizabeth, Evelyn and "Mother," and where Gene was. When the catching up was done the room fell silent for a brief moment. Perk then asked the inevitable question, "How did you know we were back here in Fluvanna?"

"Henry told me what happened to your job and about you all moving back here. "I'm so sorry," Chris replied.

The adults exchanged understanding looks as Charlie studied how the conversation was going. Chris, looking now at Jesse, continued, "I want to talk to you about that and tell you about something, but it's just for grownups."

Perk and Jesse, puzzled and a little uncomfortable looked quizzically at Chris. She nodded and smiled. Then Jesse spoke to her children, "Wayne, Gerald, Edward, your Daddy and I need to talk to Aunt Chris, so you all go on outside and play for a while now, OK? Go on now."

Perk herded the three older kids toward the door and they filed out, still dressed in nothing but their summer clothes. Jesse called out to them just as the last one cleared the door, "You all play nice now, and stay close to the house."

Charlie marveled that his little cousins didn't seem to mind the chilly dampness outside, but he stayed inside with the grownups. Chris picked up the conversation. Leaning toward Jesse and looking directly at her, Chris began to speak to Jesse and Perk, her voice soft and caring. "I know things are rough for you and the kids right now and, with cold weather and Christmas coming, we've been worried about the kids. So, we brought some things to help you get through 'til spring. We have winter clothes for all the kids. If it's alright with you, we'd like to bring them inside and put them away so the kids won't see. OK?"

Jesse was genuinely stunned. It took her a few seconds to get her senses about her. She looked at Perk, then at Charlie, then Chris. As tears wetted her eyes, she said, "Oh Chris, you shouldn't have. I don't know what to say, but thank you." She leaned over and hugged her sister-in-law tight around the neck. Chris, not used to such full, unabashed hugs, patted Jesse's back, then turned to Charlie. "Son, go out to the car and bring in those bags on the back seat for me."

Jesse turned to Perk and said, "You'll help Charlie, won't you?" Perk said he would and the two went immediately to the car. While Perk's kids ran around the yard, he and Charlie collected all the bags of clothes from the back seat and took them into the house. Chris began pulling children's clothes from a bag and showing them to Jesse.

Jesse began to cry. "Chris," she exclaimed, "you shouldn't have done all this. It's too much. We can never pay you back." At that, Perk's eyes began to get wet. Charlie and Chris got teary too.

Chris said, "The boys and I wanted to. I couldn't stand to think about those babies with no warm clothes and winter coming on. You don't have to pay it back. It's a present for you and Perk to give to your babies for Christmas."

Perk, a lump in his throat, had difficulty talking. Finally, he interjected, "I've got some work I have to get done before dark. We really appreciate what you've done for our kids, Sis. If you don't mind, while you and Jesse are going through the things you brought, I'll just slip on out and get to work."

Perk was not ungrateful. He just thought that going through the clothes was best left to the two mothers. When he turned toward the door, Charlie chimed in awkwardly, "Uh, if it's OK, Mom, I'll go help Uncle Perk - that is, if it's OK with him."

Charlie didn't want to hang around looking at children's clothes any more than Perk did.

"Sure," Perk said. "I'll be happy for you to just keep me company. You don't have to work unless you want to."

Once outside in the chilly air and dense mist, Perk and Charlie went to a shed, where Perk began collecting tools and light construction material; a hammer and handsaw, roofing nails, regular nails, two sheets of galvanized roofing tin, a few boards and a couple of rolls of fencing wire.

He put most of the material and tools in an old, rusty wheelbarrow with a half-flat tire. The rest Charlie carried in his hands while Perk wrestled the overloaded wheelbarrow to a spot on the edge of the woods away from the house. There, some posts had already been sunk, creating a rough rectangle shape formed by a tree trunk and the posts. Perk set to work building an enclosure.

Meanwhile, back in the house, Chris and Jesse went through every item Chris had bought for each child: winter shoes, goulashes and several pairs of warm socks, two changes of warm clothes, long johns, a winter coat, mittens, a cap with ear flaps and flannel pajamas.

In fairly short order Perk and Charlie, well - Perk, mostly, had built a pigpen and covered the north corner, sides and top with roofing tin, making a shelter from the weather. He then turned and headed toward the tool shed. "Come on Charlie, I need you to carry something for me."

As they walked toward the shed, Perk noticed Charlie looking back at the house, as Perk's kids filed back inside, where they were quickly sent to a bedroom to play. Perk said, "The old house has fallen into pretty rough shape since I lived here as a boy, but we'll fix it up. It'll just take a little time."

Charlie nodded but made no reply.

At the tool shed, Perk opened a heavy cardboard box. There in the bottom were three freshly-weaned piglets huddled together. They sprang to their feet when light flooded into the box. Perk picked up one of the piglets and thrust it into Charlie's chest, as it wiggled and squealed. "Here, you carry that one."

Charlie took the little fellow in his arms. Perk picked up the other two, and they started back toward the newly-built pen just as the heavy mist turned into a fine drizzle. The pink piglett with white hair and black spots seemed happy to be snuggled up in Charlie's arms. He guessed the pig was missing her mother. He unzipped his jacket and slipped the piglet inside with just its snout peeking out. "What're you gonna do with them?" Charlie asked Perk as they walked.

"Raise 'em," answered Uncle Perk.

"Are they pets for your children?"

Perk cut his eyes sideways and glanced at Charlie skeptically: "Naw, we want them to make more pigs."

"Wha-do-ya want with more pigs?" Charlie pressed.

"I guess we'll keep some, sell some, and maybe eat one or two along the way when they're grown," Perk said, matter-of-factly.

Charlie knew about slaughtering hogs. He had seen Uncle Perk and Uncle Henry do that on Granny Morris's farm: feet tied, .22 bullet to the brain, hung upside down, hair burned off, vertical slit up the belly, disemboweling . . . Charlie banished those thoughts and hugged the pink piglet tighter, reluctantly pulling her out from his jacket and putting her in the pen only when Perk told him the second time.

"There, that ought to hold 'em," declared Perk. "Come on Charlie, let's go back inside where it's warm and dry."

When Chris finished holding up each item of clothing and asking about size, fit, color and such, the kids would get one new outfit of winter clothes and shoes and a warm coat the next day, but the rest of the clothes and toys were hidden away until Santa came. When finished with all that, Chris turned to Jesse. "We brought food for the children too: non-perishables, things they'll like. I think it'll be enough to get through the winter, and a Christmas toy for each one."

Jesse again broke down in disbelief and gratitude. Chris went to the door just as Perk, and Charlie were about to come inside. "Oh. There you are. Perk, would you and Charlie help me get the boxes out of the trunk and bring them in?"

Perk answered, "Sure thing, Sis."

Chris followed Perk and Charlie to the car and opened the trunk. When Perk realized that Chris had brought food provisions for his children as well as the clothes, he was moved. He was obviously grateful and touched by his sister's gifts, but he could not hide his feelings of humiliation that his family was in the situation they were in. Seeing his expression, Chris turned to her younger brother, reached up and took him by his broad shoulders and looked him straight in the eye. When she began to speak, memories and feelings came flooding back. She was eleven and Perk seven. It was 1930, the year her father led their family back to this same farmhouse as refugees from the depression.

In that moment, she knew that the words welling up inside her were what her heart had yearned for years to say to their father. Her eyes misty, Chris said, "It isn't your fault, Perk. You're doing the best you can. You're giving those babies all the love they need, and that's more important than anything you lost in Richmond. Things will get better."

Perk could not look back at Chris as she spoke. He too was thinking about their father and the irony of his own present circumstances. Looking away, Perk nodded his head as he fought to choke back the lump in his throat. He needn't say anything. Chris saw his face and knew his mind at that moment. The boxes of non-perishable food were soon brought in, unpacked and put away.

After goodbye hugs from Jesse and the children and more thanks, Chris and Charlie went outside, climbed into the car and headed back to their little house in Lakeside. As they rode, only the hum of the engine and the "flap-flap" of the wiper blades broke the silence. Chris was still a little teary but now from happy feelings and gratitude that she could help Perk when, as an 11-year-old girl, she had been powerless to help her father and hadn't the words then to say what she felt.

Chris and Charlie arrived home with a whole new appreciation for that cozy little bungalow on Kent Street in Lakeside. For Christmas that year, there were a few gifts from friends and token gifts exchanged with Henry and his family. As agreed, no gifts were exchanged between Chris and her boys, just a Christmas card celebrating the gift of a baby called Jesus to a girl named Mary. Yet it was easily the best Christmas Chris and her boys ever had together. Gene and Charlie learned a profound truth that Chris already understood: that it is more blessed to give than to receive. And Charlie didn't eat pork for a long time.

CHAPTER 33
FUN AND GAMES

Just before that Christmas, Calvin was hired as a part-time employee at the station. He was a young veteran of the recent Korean War. He had a full-time job making cigarettes at the Phillip Morris plant. He was working at the station to make enough money to get on with his plans for marriage and a home. Calvin was steady, mild mannered, and had a friendly, boyish smile. He appeared to be in his mid-20s. He was also good-natured and seemingly a little shy.

Mahle called Calvin into the office one day and said, "Calvin, I need a part for that Packard engine re-build job. That's the pin that holds the fitch wheel to the torque arm of the power steering pressure compensator. Put $5 dollars of gas in your car on the house and go to Moores Packard, in the 900 block of the Boulevard. Try there first. If they don't have it, go to the junk auto yard out on Route-1. If they don't have it, go to Pep Boys. It's a pretty common part, so maybe a Cadillac canibbling pin would work. Try there if you have to. Hurry, 'cause I can't do anything more 'til I get that pin, ok?"

Calvin knew about making cigarettes and army guns, but nothing about car engines. He replied, "What was that?"

Male said, "Here, write it down." He handed Calvin a pad and pencil and repeated his words. Calvin wrote it down and read it back. Mahle confirmed it and sent him off. Three hours later, Calvin arrived back empty handed. When he walked into the office, Male, Chris and Joe, who was a mechanic, were in the office. Chris asked, "Well, Calvin, did you get the pin?"

"No ma'am." Calvin replied. "I went to all those places and none of them had one. The Cadillac parts department said theirs was not compatible with a Packard one and sent me to another junk car yard. I'm really sorry, but I looked everywhere."

Male smiled broadly and said, "Well son, congratulations. You've been had."

Everyone in the office burst into laughter, while Calvin stood there smiling, with confusion all over his face. Mahle explained, "There's no such thing as a "cannibling pin, or any of those other parts. It was a wild goose chase. You've been officially initiated."

With that everyone laughed and Calvin joined in, shaking his head sheepishly. All gave him a pat on the back and assured him that they had the same thing done to them when they were the newest employee.

At that time, the station did a thriving business selling fireworks. Of course fireworks had been around for a long time but had only recently been made illegal in Henrico County. They were still legal in Hanover County. Mahle saw profit in it, so he started selling the things right there at the station to people he knew.

One evening Gene and Charlie were hanging around at the station waiting for Chris to get off work. Several regular customers were there too, just talking and laughing with Chris and Calvin. While the congenial banter was carrying on, Chris left to go inside. She came out in a minute or two and rejoined the group. While Calvin was distracted, she discreetly lit a firecracker and tossed it on the ground behind him. He was totally unaware.

When the firecracker went off, Calvin took off like a startled rabbit. Though the group was laughing and calling to him to come back, he didn't stop until he was about 200 feet down Lakeside Avenue. It seems that Calvin had a mild touch of what was then called "battle fatigue." The group at the station, numbering six, had seen him jump when a car backfired but did not know the depth of his troubles.

Calvin walked back to the group with a sheepish grin on his face, and everybody had a good laugh. No one, least of all Chris, expected Calvin to run as he did. She felt a little bad about that and apologized. Calvin was quick to forgive and say it was alright. Forgiveness, however, did not mean he would not get even. A few days later when Chris was least expecting it, Calvin set off a firecracker behind her. She was as startled as he had been. Touché! The score was even.

Eventually Calvin's symptoms faded away. He matured, was promoted at Phillip Morris, got married and did not need the second job at the station any longer. As long as he worked there, Chris liked him and treated him like a younger brother. When Calvin got engaged, he proudly brought his fiancée by the station to introduce her to Chris, who, by that time, was somewhat of a Lakeside celebrity. Calvin introduced Chris as being like a big sister to him. His fiancée, for her part, was a bit star struck.

Chris's best and certainly longest enduring friendship was with Addie Johnson, who had five children. Two were girls – Betty and Helen. Betty was Gene's age. She was about five-foot- four, had light brown hair, a fair complexion, big smile, and laughed readily. Helen was Charlie's age. She was as tall as her sister and thinner. She had a medium complexion, hazel eyes, wore her hair in a ponytail and was a little shy. Although they had known each other since about age eight, now that they were teens Charlie came to appreciate her as a girl rather than as a playmate. The two mothers, perhaps wanting to relive their own adolescence, arranged a group date, chaperoned by them, of course.

The affair involved several pairs of kids. Charlie's date was Helen, since they were the youngest at 14 years old. They didn't have a clue what to do or how to act, since it was their first date e-v-e-r! Chris had tried to prepare Charlie, but the social manners she told him about seemed to Charlie to be a hundred years old. Gene had invited a girl that he liked, and Betty's designated blind date was Bootsy LeFon. He was middle son of Dr. Jerry LeFon, the family doctor to most everyone in Lakeside it seemed. Bootsy was Gene's age, had wavy brown hair, fair complexion with cheeks that looked rosy most of the time, and a propensity for mischief.

During the movie, Charlie noticed that Bootsy and Gene had put their arms around their dates' shoulders. So he overcame his bashfulness and put his arm around Helen's. To his surprise and delight Helen cuddled a little closer. The armrest thwarted any closer cuddling. When the mindless teen-age movie ended, the whole entourage went to a Shoneys restaurant on west Broad Street.

The other kids, by prior secret scheme, all piled into one semi-circular booth, leaving hapless and unaware Helen and Charlie to sit at a table, alone, but in plain view of the other kids. It was like dinner theater, only Charlie and Helen were on stage and the others were the audience. This development added immensely to their already-heightened self-consciousness, especially when the other kids started teasing them.

Chris and Addie thought the whole thing was just too sweet, especially with Helen and Charlie sitting alone together. They thought the two looked a little like a Norman Rockwell painting of sorts. How romantic!

Bootsy said, "Don't they look soooo cute. I bet they order one strawberry milkshake and two straws."

That is exactly what Charlie was going to do. Scratch that idea and hope he has enough money for two shakes.

Gene chimed in, "Oh yeah, we can see under your table, so don't be playin' footsie over there. And no kissin' either."

Bootsy added salt to the gaping wound. "Oh Helen, your heart-throb Charlie is already going steady with the ugliest girl in his homeroom. They make out in the janitor's closet, with all the mops and brooms. When they come out they smell like Lysol."

All of this was bogus, of course, and Helen knew that. Still, Charlie wanted to crawl under the table.

Addie interceded in her calm way. "That's enough now. You boys leave Helen and Charlie alone."

Chris added, "You kids should mind your manners, like Helen and Charlie. You don't hear them making fun of you."

Helen just sat there, trying to look like she was having fun. She whispered to Charlie, "It's alright. Don't pay any attention to them. We can have fun by ourselves."

Charlie smiled sickly and tried to go with Helen's advice. For Helen and him, though, it was a monumental embarrassment. Worse than that, it was an excruciating humiliation. Charlie felt like a nerd, a dweeb, and a twerp, all rolled up into a pathetic teen jerk.

Helen felt sorrier for Charlie than she did for herself, which turned out to be a good thing for him. When her compassion later turned into affection, they had a brief boyfriend-girlfriend thing going. Being 14 and humiliated in public by your peers has its rewards. Charlie's dating life had only one way to go. It had to get better, and it did.

CHAPTER 34
SUITORS

After her divorce from Emmett, Chris attracted the attention of would-be suitors. It didn't matter whether she tried to or not. They just came. Like I said, she was very pretty in her youth and middle years. The list of wanna-be's included Scotty, who was Perk's army buddy, a country music singer and songwriter, a building contractor, a manager for a new car dealership, a businessman.

It must be said, too, that much of the male attention Chris received was not welcomed and certainly not invited. It is an unfortunate truth that, in her job she was subjected to everything from lewd jokes spoken in her hearing, to sexually suggestive teasing, and on occasion, worse. It was not from employees, but from a few customers.

Sometimes these affronts happened while Gene or Charlie was present, as if the would-be-suitor thought the boys were too stupid to understand what was going on - or he couldn't care less. These incidents left the boys feeling outraged and helpless.

Charlie sometimes seethed with rage and feelings of powerlessness to protect his mom. More than once he entertained the fantasy of being a grownup and knocking the offending male silly with a punch to the face. He even talked about it with Chris. He asked her why she put up with it. Her answer reflected the plight of many women, single or married, who had to work for a living.

With a tinge of anger seeping into her tone, Chris answered simply, "Leave it alone. It comes with the job, and I have to put up with it to make a living. That's just the way it is. I can take care of myself."

Gene, for his part felt as Charlie did, but he was more sage about it and understood their mother's dilemma without having to be told.

There were some decent men who came along, men who showed gentlemanly interest in Chris – single guys with good manners who respected and admired her. For the most part, though, she basically did not have the time or energy for a romantic relationship. Looking at her prodigious work schedule and the demands of raising two boys, it is easy to see why. There were precious few times when Chris went out on a date. Most of the time, she was polite but developed no real interest in the few fellows with whom she did go out.

In early 1954, a nice looking businessman in a suit and driving a very nice car became a regular customer at the station. His name was Brad. He was impressed with Chris right away. After they had gotten to know each other, Brad invited Chris out for dinner. He had been widowed about a year before he met her, and he was raising a son, Todd, who was about two years younger than Charlie.

Brad was a gentleman and treated Chris like a lady. That relationship flourished, and Chris, who was naturally upbeat and cheerful most of the time, was more so. When they were teasing each other, she called him Screwball, and he called her, Toots. They often included their children in their outings. Gene and Charlie liked Todd, and they blended well together.

Months passed as their relationship flourished. Eventually Brad began to talk about a long-term future together. For the first time since Emmett, Chris was receptive. She began to hint to Gene and Charlie about having a "younger brother."

Brad was ready to marry. He talked to Chris about not having to work, about staying home and taking care of the house and raising their three boys. It sounded wonderful to Chris though she honestly told Brad she had a lot of thinking to do before giving him an answer to his proposal.

Soon after that conversation, Brad's company advised him he was getting a promotion and a sizable pay raise, but he would be transferred to the company's headquarters in Tampa, Florida. He wanted to marry Chris right away and move them and the three boys down there. He told her how terrific it would be without cold, snowy winters; that with his raise they would buy a terrific house with all new furnishings and Chris would have all the things a woman dreams of having.

Chris thought it sounded wonderful, almost like a dream come true. She even asked Gene and Charlie how they would like to live in sunny Florida, with no cold winters, and she could be just a mom and take care of them and their home.

Gene and Charlie liked Todd, and they both wondered what life would be like living in Tampa but fretted about giving up their friends in Lakeside. Soon, their conflicted feelings tilted toward acceptance of the move, and their excitement about a new life began to grow. Then, Mother Nature provided a powerful reason to think on it a little more.

In mid-October that year, an epic tropical storm, Hurricane Hazel, came roaring out of the Caribbean. It killed over a thousand people in Haiti before moving on to ravage the west coast of Florida and leave a swath of destruction through Georgia, the Carolinas, Virginia and points north.

The forecast called for the storm to strike Richmond in the afternoon. Around midday, with early storm clouds scudding across the blue sky and gusty winds beginning to pick up, the schools closed and sent all their students home to ride out the coming killer storm.

Gene and Charlie went home like everybody else . . . but that doesn't mean they stayed there. Chris had heard about the school closing and called the boys to make sure they were at home and told them to stay inside. They promised they would, but then they didn't want to miss anything exciting. After all, they had never seen a real hurricane before.

After playing in the street with Gene for a while, Charlie went over to his buddy Booties house on Kenmore Road at the corner of Westlake. Bryan Park was just two blocks away, so the two of them walked to the park to watch the trees blow down. They took up residence in a picnic shelter that had stone walls on each end, a heavy, log-roof structure and was open on the sides. They stayed there as the howling winds came blasting out of the east.

After a good amount of time, the truly exhilarating winds began to subside. Soon the clouds broke up, the sun came out and the winds all but disappeared. Charlie and Bootsy left the shelter and walked through the park checking out the downed trees and limbs. Soon they had seen enough and started back to Charlie's house, eight blocks north of the park.

As they meandered toward Kent Street, the clouds quickly returned and the wind began to howl again, but this time it came blasting out of the west. What Charlie and Bootsy thought was the end of the storm was actually the eye. No matter. They just continued their play in the street in front of Charlie's house.

The westerly winds were blowing about 100 right down Kent Street. Bootsy and Charlie, joined by Gene, soon figured out that if they held their jackets open like a sail, then ran with the wind and jumped up, they could break the world record for the long jump.

When the storm was over for real, Bootsy went home, and the three were none the worse for wear. Though their parents were a little miffed, Gene, Charlie and Bootsy enjoyed an excellent adventure and gained a valuable understanding of hurricanes.

When it came time to fish or cut bait, Chris turned down Brad's proposal. It could be that she decided to stay in Virginia because she didn't want to live where hurricanes were a constant threat, or it could be that Hazel served as a reality check about how stormy marriages can get. Whatever the reason, she decided to swim in the pond that she had landed in.

Her closest friends agreed that she probably just couldn't bring herself to be dependent on a man again, especially when it meant moving 800 miles away from her friends and family, and from the career she loved. Besides, she didn't have to marry again. She had proven to everyone, especially to herself, that she was able to get along just fine on her own.

Brad was disappointed and a little hurt, but he asked her to give it some time. They promised to stay in touch and see each other when they could; and maybe she would change her mind. After Brad moved to Florida, he and Chris did keep in touch for a while, and they saw each other on his infrequent business trips to Richmond. But the long-distance relationship eventually wore itself out. That was the last time Chris considered marriage. She had discovered her true self, and she was content with the woman she found.

CHAPTER 35

FUNDAMENTALS

After Brad moved to Florida, Chris settled back into the life she had built for herself in Lakeside with her two sons. There, she was independent, successful, well-liked, respected and even admired by a wide circle of people from many walks in life. She just continued on working and seeing to it that she took care of the essentials in her children's development.

Dunking, Acorns and a Crusade

Chris had Gene and Charlie join Boy Scout Troop 40, sponsored by Hatcher Memorial Baptist Church. Though Chris went to church only on special occasions, she held firmly to her Christian faith. In the summer of 1954, the Billy Graham Crusade came to Richmond. One of Chris's customer friends invited her, Gene and Charlie to attend the crusade with her family. Chris had to work as usual, but she wanted Gene and Charlie to go.

Chris didn't order her boys to go, but she did extend the offer and encouraged them. Charlie accepted the offer and went. He was deeply moved by Billy's sermon and wanted to go forward at the altar call. Charlie was afraid he wouldn't find his way back to the family he was with, so he did not join the throng cascading out of the bleachers. He did, however, join in the prayer that followed, led by Graham himself.

Even though she didn't succeed in getting them to go to church and Sunday school regularly, Chris insisted that Gene and Charlie attend classes to prepare for baptism. Being baptized was the natural and expected result of the classes. Both boys were baptized in the baptismal pool in the original sanctuary of Hatcher Memorial Church by Dr. William Lumpkin.

Gene and Charlie had met Dr. Lumpkin earlier. They and other Scouts in Troop 40 were in the churchyard learning to build ladders, shelters and other useful things using nothing but twine, a pocket knife and sapling tree trunks. At the time, mature oak trees in the yard were dropping thousands of acorns. That meant a ferocious acorn battle would eventually ensue, and it did.

What was not expected was Dr. Lumpkin coming out and joining in the fight. The free-for-all quickly turned into a kids-against-adults, there being but one of the latter. He was big, powerful and accurate, with a throwing arm like a major league pitcher. When he targeted one of the kids, he didn't miss. A little brown projectile he hurled struck Charlie's back like a hornet sting and left a whelp to prove it. That day, Charlie learned that preachers are not sissies but are regular people, and some of them can throw acorns like pro baseball pitchers.

The Ethos of Work

Gene and Charlie had been introduced to light household chores back on Idlewood Avenue-such things as taking out the trash, emptying cinders from the Warm Morning cast iron stove in the kitchen that heated the whole place and refilling the coal scuttle with lump coal from the shed out back.

Now in Lakeside, they had to pick up more of the load. That included mowing the grass, weeding the borders, trimming shrubs, putting out the trash and retrieving the cans after the county truck emptied them, washing the dishes, carrying in and putting away the groceries, sometimes dusting and sweeping the house, changing linens on the beds and cleaning the bathroom.

They were less than reliable at first, but they grew in dependability as they grew in years. Beginning when they were about eleven, Chris paid them an allowance that started at 50 cents per week. As they grew, it was increased to a dollar a week until they were working for money outside their home.

Friends of Chris would occasionally ask if they could "borrow" one or both of her boys for a project or a day. Chris, of course, always said yes. The boys cleaned gutters, trimmed shrubs, mowed lawns, moved furniture and did other menial labor. Sometimes they just did it to help. Other times it was for pay.

By the time they were 13, they were no strangers to the principle that useful work is both financially rewarding and fulfilling. It actually made them feel good to do something constructive and beneficial; maybe they felt a little pride or a sense of accomplishment, or maybe relief from boredom. Probably what they felt was a little of all of those.

As Gene and then Charlie reached age 12, Chris had them doing jobs at the station, for which they got 50-cents an hour. The work included washing and vacuuming cars, cleaning tools, washing windows, cleaning the customer lounge and bathrooms and wiping up grease and oil spills. If they complained that the task was too hard, Chris would say, "Put a little elbow grease into it. Then you'll be able to do it."

On one occasion, Charlie was invited for a weekend at the river with Bootsy and his family to help with a project. Charlie was glad to help and eager to go to the river and hang out with Bootsy.

The project was seriously hard labor, and dangerous. It involved erecting a bulkhead along the foot of an embankment that ran along the river front of their property. Storm tides and winds were cutting into the embankment, causing a part of the backyard to drop into the river.

The bulkhead was made by setting large concrete pipe sections side by side. Each pipe section was four feet in diameter and about four feet long which meant they weighed something on the order of 500 pounds each. They could be rolled pretty easily over hard, flat ground. The problem was how to keep them from going out of control as they were rolled down the embankment. The solution was to use heavy rope anchored to a tree, with block and tackle pulleys to ease the things down to where they were set in place.

They got the job done without mishap, but Charlie was a bit apprehensive when Booty's dad told him to climb down the bank below the concrete pipe and push back against it to help keep it from off course. It's fair to say that Charlie gave some thought to the question, "What if the rope breaks?" If it had, it is certain Charlie would not have lived to tell about it.

When he got back home he complained to Chris about the project. She listened attentively, then shrugged and replied, "Well, you're here aren't you? A little heavy labor never hurt anyone. Sometimes a little danger is just part of the job."

It may seem a bit callous for her to say that, but it was not a thoughtless remark. The way Chris explained things to Gene and Charlie it would not have helped them grow into men of courage and character if she had deprived them of experiencing hard, even slightly hazardous work. That lesson was well learned by both of her sons.

Emergency Response

Lakeside Avenue was a major corridor for commuter traffic between the suburbs and the city. In the evening rush hour, the traffic was thick at the intersection of Lakeside and Dumbarton Road, where the station was situated. That place saw the worst of the accidents on Lakeside Avenue.

Pedestrians trying to cross Lakeside there were sometimes hit by moving cars. When that happened, Chris usually heard the screech of tires and the blare of a horn, quickly followed by the dull thump of steel against flesh and bone.

One night, in the fall of 1955, a man tried to cross Lakeside Avenue in the crosswalk but did not wait for the light to turn red. Chris happened to be standing in front of the station talking to Calvin. As soon as she heard the familiar "honk – screech – thump," Chris looked out and saw a man lying on the pavement, bathed in the headlights of the car that had hit him. The man started to stand up, but then one leg collapsed and he fell backward to the pavement with a scream of pain.

Chris ran out to him. He had what looked like a second knee bent at 45 degrees, between his ankle and natural knee. The man, dazed and confused, tried again to sit up. "Stay down," Chris told him. "You were hit by a car. You're hurt. I'll get an ambulance and help you, but you have to be still. Do you understand?"

The man looked into her face, recognized her and became calm. He lay back and closed his eyes. Chris yelled, pleading with the onlookers who were doing nothing but gawking. "Will someone call the police and get an ambulance here? This man needs medical help."

Next she called out to Calvin to bring her several clean shop rags, then returned her attention to the stricken man, who was in terrible pain. Though he continued to lie still with eyes closed, every 20 to 30 seconds he opened them and looked to make sure Chris was still there at his side. Then he closed them again.

Back at the station, Calvin quickly grabbed several clean shop rags and gave them to Charlie, who was working there. Charlie delivered them to Chris on a dead run. When he reached his mother's side, he could see that the injured man's "extra" knee had bloody bone sticking through the skin and the fabric of his trousers, with blood gushing out of his pant cuff.

Chris wasted no time. She took the pants in her hands and ripped the seam from the cuff to the knee. She fashioned a tourniquet with a clean shop rag, which she twisted tight using the small screwdriver she carried in her uniform shirt pocket. She then gingerly covered the gaping wound with the other clean shop rags. When she had done what she could, she sat down on the pavement and comforted the man, cradling his head in her lap until the ambulance arrived. During that whole incident, other witnesses and bystanders did nothing to help unless Chris asked them do a specific task. It was a pattern that repeated itself.

Chris never seemed to give any thought to being a leader. Driven by her compassion for others, she always had the presence of mind to size up a situation quickly, see what needed to be done and had the courage to step up and do it. By her example, and by involving Gene and Charlie in crisis situations, they learned how to be calm, proactive and effective in emergency situations — a lesson that proved valuable in later years.

Not long after this incident, yet another newspaper story came out featuring Chris, branding her "the Florence Nightingale of Lakeside." During this time, she became actively involved in the local chapter of the American Red Cross, volunteering her time and labor, as well as Gene and Charlie's, to work on various emergency relief projects. Chris continued as an active Red Cross volunteer until she was no longer able to do it.

Community Service

In the fall of 1955, torrential rains inundated Virginia from Richmond to the Blue Ridge Mountains. Experience had shown that flooding in low lying areas of Richmond would soon follow, as the massive runoff made its way to the sea. Houses which at that time sat down along the floodplain of the creek that crosses under Lakeside Avenue just north of the S-curve, were sure to be flooded unless something was done to protect them.

The Henrico County Police and Fire Departments and the Red Cross put out the call for volunteers to help build a sandbag levee between the houses and the creek. Cub Scouts, Boy Scouts, military reservists, and a small army of civilian Lakesiders arrived, as did dump-truck loads of sand, hundreds of bundles of sandbags, dozens of shovels, portable generators and flood lamps, along with a Red Cross coffee and donut wagon, plus reporters and cameramen from the local TV stations.

Chris suggested to Gene and Charlie that they come help since she was going down there herself to pitch in. It was the proverbial offer they could not refuse. Along with many other volunteers, Chris, Gene and Charlie began filling and placing sandbags at about 4:00 p.m. that afternoon.

After about six hours of backbreaking labor, Chris retired to the Red Cross wagon and helped out there. The boys continued working on the sandbags until the crest of the flood passed and the waters began to recede. It was 3:00 a.m. the next day when it was over.

Gene and Charlie, like everybody else who was there, felt a wave of satisfaction and a little pride that they had saved the homes of their fellow Lakesiders, and they were exhausted. As they rode home in Chris's car, Gene said, "I'm so tired I can hardly move. I think I'll sleep 'til noon at least."

Charlie added his concurring sentiments, but Chris had another whole thought in mind.

"You can't sleep in," she said. "Tomorrow is a school day. You have to get up and go at the regular time."

"Oh Mom . . . !" Charlie protested in disbelief. "All the other kids who helped said their parents were letting them stay home from school today. It isn't fair to make us go."

Chris rebutted, "I'm sure most other parents won't let their kids stay home today. I'm not responsible for the other kids, just you two, and your education is more important than you sleeping in. It isn't going to hurt you. You're going to school, so if I were you I'd get to bed as soon as I could."

Once home, the boys wasted no time getting in their beds. They were asleep in about a half-minute. Sure enough, Chris set her alarm, woke up and made sure Gene and Charlie got up and out the door in time for school. She decided that since she was up anyway, she might as well stay up. She got herself ready and went to work early. With that experience in emergency volunteer work, Chris taught her boys the joy and deep satisfaction that comes from voluntary community involvement. And they also found out they were able do a lot more than they thought they could, and that getting only three or four hours of sleep occasionally was no big deal - a lesson that served them well in years to come.

Integrity

When Charlie got home after dinner one evening, Chris scolded him for being late and for not calling to tell her where he was and what he was doing. She explained once again how important it was to be dependable. Then she told him to go eat the dinner she had kept warm in the oven for him. He explained that he had been hanging out with Woody Woodson, said he was sorry, then added that he had already eaten.

She asked where. He told her Shoney's. She asked how he paid for it. She knew he was broke until the next payday. Charlie said he borrowed enough from his March of Dimes charity collections that afternoon to buy a burger, fries and a shake. He said he would pay the money back in two days when he got paid for his part-time work.

Chris was aghast. She spoke to him in an urgent voice that brought Gene into the room to find out what was going on. She explained to Gene what had happened, then told Charlie that he must never, ever do such a thing again; that borrowing from other people's money entrusted to him and doing it without their knowledge was dishonest, that it always leads to stealing. She was emphatic and said she had seen that sort of thing before by a former customer. The customer borrowed a little here, a little there, from his boss's money, and he soon owed more money than he could pay back; that he was caught, convicted of embezzling and now had a permanent criminal record after spending time in jail.

Charlie protested that it was harmless because it was a small amount, that he already had money due him that he would get in two days. Chris was adamant, saying that embezzling always starts with borrowing a small amount but invariably escalates. There must never be an exception to the rule. She lent Charlie the amount he had borrowed, and he replaced the coins in the March of Dimes folders. In two days' time, he got his pay at work and repaid Chris.

That stern talk from their mother made a deep impression on both Gene and Charlie. They began for the first time to understand that financial integrity is of the highest importance, that corners must never be cut. That lesson took and was a guiding principle that served them well.

CHAPTER 36
CREATIVE PROBLEM SOLVING

Dick Mahle's station had well over 100 feet of paved apron fronting on Lakeside Avenue, with no sidewalk, curb or gutter. The street pavement and the driveway just butted up against each other. That left a lot of room for cars to come and go.

The only obstruction along the frontage was a utility pole that sat about midway along the front property line. That was a good place for it, because it wasn't actually in the path of customers coming and going. It also served as a stopping point for buses because people just naturally tended to gather around that pole to wait for the bus.

One day a county truck showed up and installed a metal pole with a bus stop sign right there along Lakeside Avenue. Instead of placing the sign next to the utility pole, the spot they chose was directly in the path of most cars exited the station's driveway near Bumbarton Road.

When the workmen started putting in the pole, Mahle walked out and explained to them that it was an obstruction and was likely to cause an accident. He suggested they put it next to the utility pole where the busses had been stopping for years. The workmen simply shrugged and said they had to put it where they were told.

Mahle got the name and number of their boss, went back inside and called the official responsible for the sign. Nice try, but no luck. He got nowhere.

Many customer questions and complaints later, Mahle called the county again, and again it was to no avail. Later that day, he was growling about it again to Chris. When he had finished letting off steam, she said with a sly grin, "I can get that sign moved."

He turned toward her with a skeptical but curious look and asked, "How are you gonna to do that? I've already called every-body and tried everything, and I got nowhere."

Chris just smiled and replied in a playful tone, "Oh, just wait a little while." Then she walked away, leaving Mahle standing there scratching his head and trying to figure out what she was conjur-ing up.

Late one afternoon three weeks later, Chris answered a call from a female customer whose car wouldn't start. She needed a jump or a tow. Chris said she'd be right there, hung up, and head-ed out to the service truck. Mahle asked, "Where are you going in such an all-fired hurry?"

"On a service call, Mildred Collins has a dead battery," Chris said as she kept walking.

"Why don't you let one of the boys go? You don't have to han-dle something as simple as that," Mahle called after her.

"I need to handle this one," she shouted back as she reached for the truck's door handle.

Mahle didn't understand at all. He stood there perplexed, then shook his head and walked back into the office as the truck rumbled to life and started rolling toward the street.

As he walked, his back to the street, he was brought to a sudden stop when he heard the service truck's engine revving up, accom-panied by "crunch," and the sound of metal hitting the pavement. He turned and looked. Of all the bad luck, right there in front of the station, Chris had an accident with the service truck, the one with the big, flat, wide, heavy, custom steel bumper. Why, she ran right over that silly bus stop sign and bent it flat to the ground. The truck? It didn't even get a scratch.

Mahle's mouth dropped open, then he chuckled, shook his head and said, "I'll be damned if that don't beat all." As he watched, Chris just kept going and handled the service call. When she returned a half hour later she called the police, who came and investigated the accident.

Chris explained, "The glare of the sun shining down Dumbarton Road kept me from seeing that sign pole. It's brand new, and I wasn't used to it being there. For years the sign was on the telephone pole over there. Moving it to a pole over here doesn't seem to make much sense, does it, officer?"

"It doesn't make a lot of sense to me either," said the officer.

Chris continued, "Thank God no one was waiting for a bus. Putting that sign there is dangerous. Somebody needs to tell the county streets and roads department to move that sign back over there, where it's always been."

The police officer jotted down notes as she talked. The official police report noted that the sign was placed in a dangerous spot that obstructed the flow of traffic in and out of the business. It didn't hurt that Chris knew and was well respected by all the Henrico policemen who patrolled Lakeside.

A few days later workmen came, removed the broken pole and sign and asked Chris where she would like them to put the new one. Chris said, "Put it over there," pointing to the utility pole where Mahle had told them to put it in the first place.

"Yes, Ma'am," they answered.

As the workmen headed back out to the street, Mahle smiled and muttered to himself "How does she come up with stuff like that?"

Chris explained, "I figured that me driving the truck over the sign pole was what some customer would do sooner or later, and it made sense for me to do it with the truck than for a customer's car to be damaged and the customer maybe hurt."

That same year, a week or two before Christmas, a sleet and freezing rainstorm left trees coated with a layer of ice. Evergreen trees in particular looked like something from a fantasy winter wonderland. Chris spray-painted her blue spruce Christmas tree with silver paint with a hint of blue mixed in. It turned out to look very much like those ice-encrusted evergreens she had seen. After ornaments and all-white lights, she added the traditional silvery tinsel. The tree shimmered, its fragrance filling the room. Her family and friends loved it.

She decorated another small tree the same way for the station. When it was displayed, the customers admired it. Next thing you know painted trees became standard in Chris's home and many others in Lakeside for a string of Christmases.

At one point she wanted to buy a comfortable office-style sofa for the customer lounge. Not finding one suitable for the station, she went out and bought the materials, built a sturdy wood frame, made the cushions and upholstered them in "Naugahide" by herself at home. Naugahide is an early form of "pleather," or plastic that looks and feels like leather. The sofa looked just like it had come from an expensive office furniture store. Mahle's first reaction when he saw it was one of amazement that she had built it herself, but he finally had to admit that he was pleased. He asked her, "How did you know how to build it?"

Chris answered with a grin, "A little birdie told me."

Actually, she just turned over her own sofa at home and looked at how the frame was built and copied it. She already knew about upholstering car seats, so there was nothing to that. To her, building a sofa was a piece of cake.

CHAPTER 37
SALVAGE CARS AND TEENS

Gene turned 16 in December, 1953. Not long after that, Chris found a 1937 Dodge two door business coupe that she bought as salvage. She rebuilt the engine, repaired the rust and dents, sprayed on a new coat of paint, and gave it to her boys, though only Gene was licensed to drive. It had room for only two passengers, unless a third one was a girl in her boyfriend's lap. The running boards, though, could "safely" carry two more. So, the Dodge became a stagecoach travelling between Hermitage High and home, and offering free rides for his friends. Gene and Charlie had a little difficulty deciding what sort of teens they wanted to be. At first, Gene took up with some friends who were a bit rough around the edges, and Charlie was allowed to tag along. Some of those and Charlie were the ones riding the running boards of Kent Street Overland Stage Company.

The Dodge, sadly, lost its life one night in a tragic accident when a utility pole jumped off the curb and ran headlong into the front of the car. Chris was in the hospital for a few days having a routine operation in her belly. Charlie, though he had no driver's license, was accused of being the driver, but he steadfastly proclaimed his innocence. Gene would just as soon wreak his displeasure with his fists upon his hapless younger brother. Fortunately, his impulse was restrained by Chris's better judgment.

The true culprit was Bootsy Le Fon, and he readily admitted it. Charlie's only involvement in that crash was inviting friends over to his house for an underage drinking party on a rainy night, letting Bootsy drive Gene's Lakeside stage while under the influence of whisky, and riding in the shotgun seat. He told all involved adults that he was, for those reasons, completely absolved of any fault. The poor lad had not heard of "accessory before the fact." But for Charlie's own missteps Bootsy would never have been behind the wheel that night, nor drinking whisky.

For a replacement, Chris salvaged the body of a 1939 Plymouth four door sedan, medium blue, brown interior, with working radio. It was in great shape inside and out except for the engine. That had thrown a piston rod through the engine block. For Chris, it was a simple task to pull the engine out of the totaled Dodge and mount it up in the Plymouth. Gene was in wheels again. For some unknown reasons, the back rest supports for the front seat soon broke, as if someone had been trying really hard to lay back in it. When that happened, just resting your back against it caused the thing to just flop backward to about ten degrees shy of horizontal. Gene used a stick to prop it up, one end stuck into the ashtray slot in the back of the seat, the other end wedged between the floorboard and the base of the back seat.

One night during the summer before his junior year at Hermitage High, Charlie, 16 and newly licensed, was out with several of those edgy boys that Gene and he hung out with- Wimpy, Wade and Al. Wimpy had already dropped out of school and the other two seemed like they were headed that way too.

Charlie was driving the Plymouth, with Wade in the jump seat and Wimpy and Al in the back. As he drove, they kept jerking the stick out, causing the front backrest to fall. Charlie repeatedly told them not to do that because it could cause an accident. Charlie was growing more demanding as they continued their antics. They promised they'd stop, and Charlie drove on without incident to Bill's Barbecue on West Broad.

About 11:30 p.m., the group left Bill's in good spirits, with their stomachs filled with hamburgers, greasy shoestring fries and Pepsi Cola. Traffic was light on Staples Mill Road as they headed toward Lakeside. The boys talked enthusiastically about the really cute girls they had flirted with at Bill's and about the "really cool" hot rod that had rumbled through Bill's parking lot revving its engine, looking for a drag race.

A little way down Staples Mill Road, maybe three-quarters of a mile, Wade asked Charlie a question. Charlie began to answer. In the middle of his sentence, he saw Wade signal Wimpy, who jerked the stick out again. The seat back and Charlie fell backward, nearly sending the car out of control. All three of those guys laughed hysterically. That was one jerk too many; or three, depending on which jerks you're talking about.

Charlie had already been thinking hard about his friendship with these fellows. Now he was mad enough to fight any of them that wanted a go at him. He jammed on the brakes, propelling them forward off their seats. In the angriest, loudest state they had ever witnessed from him, Charlie got out of the car and yanked the rear driver's side door open.

"Alright! That's it! I've had all I'm gonna take from ya'll. I told you over and over not to do that, but you kept on. You don't give a damn about me or my car, even if you caused an accident and somebody got hurt. Get out!"

Wade, Wimpy and Al just sat there, mouths open, looking at Charlie. They'd never seen that side of him and didn't know how serious he was.

"NOW!," Charlie demanded, "I'm not carryin' you another foot. Get out or I'll drag your worthless asses out myself!"

Wade, smiling and trying to laugh it off, said, "But it's at least three miles to my house, four to Wimpy and Al's. Come on, Charlie. Get back in. I swear we won't do that any more."

"Wade, ya'll promised me at least five times that you wouldn't do it again, and you kept right on. I don't care if it's five miles. The walk won't hurt you. Now get out of my car!"

This time the three boys scrambled out. Charlie thought they might be getting out to fight him, and he was only too happy to have a chance to vent his anger with his fists on their faces. Instead, they just closed the car doors and stood aside, blank-faced, as Charlie got back in and drove off. He never called them or saw them again, to Chris's great satisfaction.

That episode was the catalyst that resolved his mixed feelings. Charlie realized those friends were a little too wild, too prone to street fights and malicious mischief. Those guys were frankly too unmotivated and without direction for him.

Gene had already found interests elsewhere, like a girl named Patricia, who lived two doors down the street. Still, Gene continued his friendship with that bunch for a while, until Patricia, his ham radio hobby and a part time job took up all his time.

Gene seemed always to be on the side of the underdog, except where his pesky brother was concerned. Seriously though, Gene did lean toward the less popular- those who were teased, picked on or bullied. They were more sincere and genuine than those who seemed to always populate the thrones of Hermitage High's homecoming kings, queens and their royal courts.

Gene's homeroom teacher was fresh out of college, young, sweet and totally unprepared for a certain obstreperous boy in her homeroom who seemed to be on a mission to make her life as miserable as possible. On one occasion he succeeded in bringing the poor neophyte teacher to tears. That did it.

Gene had been smoldering for several weeks over that kid's treatment of the teacher. He got out from his seat, walked up to Mr. Obnoxious, looked down at him in disgust, then picked up the boy's desk with him still sitting in it and threw them both about six feet through the air and into the concrete block wall. It seems that Gene inherited Emmett's eye-popping physical strength.

That boy never again pestered the teacher. After a long talk with the principal, George Moody, who applauded his intent but not his action, Gene accepted his kind recommendation that he leave the school. He left with the great admiration and regrets of many teachers.

He eventually took a GED exam cold turkey and scored 90-something. Gene took that certificate and grade sheet to Mr. Moody, who had in the meantime become superintendent of Henrico Schools. When he saw Gene's grade he awarded him his Henrico County high school diploma on the spot. Gene then went on active duty in the military.

Soon after ending his friendship with Wade, Wimpy and Al, Charlie quit smoking and traded his black leather jacket, tee-shirt, dirty blue jeans and slicked-backed hair for tan khaki trousers, penny loafers, and button-down-collar shirts with rolled up cuffs. To go with that, he sported a flat-top haircut. You might say he adopted the Joe College look, as that style was called. He then aligned himself with Woody Woodson, who was college-bound, older than Charlie but younger than Gene.

Like Gene and Charlie, Woody had been on the fringe of the Wade, Wimpy, Al bunch, but he was also steering away from them. Besides, Woody had a younger sister, Harriett, who was pretty and very popular at John Marshall High. She was another reason for Charlie to befriend Woody.

At summer's end, Woody was to start his senior year at John Marshall. He was talking about colleges and to which ones he would send applications. Charlie was enjoying just being a rising junior and his still-new association with the clean-cut set in his class at Hermitage High. He even managed to get dates with some of the most popular girls. He figured they went out with him be-cause he was a novelty.

CHAPTER 38
FINDING THE FUTURE

Back in school that fall as a junior, Charlie began to study in earnest, something he had never done. Though he had made a dramatic change, he was in a stew about what to do after graduating from Hermitage High. He liked the idea of the military partly because his dad was a career National Guardsman and partly because he liked the idea of a uniform and discipline. He decided to join the Navy Reserve. With Chris signing the papers, he did. In October he started attending monthly drills. There he learned the basics of wearing a uniform, when and when not to salute, spit-polishing his new Navy issue shoes, marching and standing guard. He loved it.

During spring semester Charlie learned that he could do Honor Roll work. His teachers took notice of the change and began to encourage him. One Saturday morning Charlie was out in the front yard mowing the grass and still stewing and about what to do after graduation. The real world was rapidly approaching. In one more school year it would be upon him. He was having second thoughts about a career as an enlisted Navy man.

Meanwhile, Gene had taken a job with Davey Tree Company. They would plant or take down trees, prune and feed them, and treat them if they were diseased. The job was very demanding, involved a lot of climbing, pulling and lifting. In the summer of 1957, the tree company had a major job near the town of Bassett, Virginia. When he returned home at summer's end, the pimple-faced restless boy had become a man. His face was clear, and his well-tanned body was ripped. His muscles even seemed to have muscles. He had gained self-confidence as well as marketable job skills in a useful trade.

In Charlie's case, his uncertainty, confusion and conflicted feelings all coalesced into clarity. He was unhappy with his life as it was and unhappy with the choices he had been mulling over. The only way to make himself happy was to set goals that would bring him the respect he needed, a career he loved, a nice home and enough income to keep from living payday to payday. Above all, he wanted to make his mother proud.

In the early part of the following fall semester, Charlie's senior year, he was at home doing his homework in the bedroom that he once had shared with Gene. Chris, still in her khaki work uniform, had been home long enough to wash up and put dinner on to cook. She went to the living room and called out, "Charlie, come sit down son. I want to talk to you."

That usually meant trouble, but at this stage of his life Charlie could not imagine what trouble would cause her to call for a mother-son talk. He found her sitting on the sofa. He sat down in a chair facing her. He was more than a little curious, and a tad anxious. Looking directly at him Chris went straight to the point. "Son, do you want to go to college?"

Charlie was caught totally off guard. He needed to think, to tune his mind to the topic of the question. "Ma'am?", he said even though he'd heard her plainly.

She repeated, "Do you want to go to college?"

Charlie broke eye contact and said, "We can't afford anything like that, Mom."

"But is that something you want to do?" Chris pressed.

Charlie hesitated for a pensive moment, looked down and answered as if he were admitting to doing something wrong, "I guess so," he said weakly.

He had indeed thought about it, and Chris could see that his "I guess so" was a marshmallow way of saying what should have been a rock solid "Yes."

"Why didn't you tell me so we could talk about it?" she asked.

Growing more uncomfortable, Charlie looked about the room, everywhere but toward his mother. She patiently waited in silence. He finally looked down and said with resignation, "I didn't think there was any use in doing that."

"What do you mean? That's no reason," Chris persisted.

Still looking down, Charlie said, "I just don't want to put any more burden on you, Mom. You've worked so hard . . ." Charlie's unfinished sentence hung in the air.

Chris saw that he could not get the rest of his words out. She spoke in all sincerity, "Son, with the Lord's help, you can do anything you want to do if you set your mind to it. If that's what you want, I'll find a way to help pay for it. I'll talk to the bank and see what they can do. But you're gonna have to help too. OK?"

Charlie protested, "But Mom . . ."

"No buts," Chris cut him off. "Do you know how long I've prayed for you and your brother . . . what a dream come true it would be for me if you go to college? I want you to do it if want it bad enough to see it through. I'll help pay for it as long as I am healthy enough to work, and you get a degree that will earn a living."

Charlie then realized how much it meant to her and warmed up to what she had laid out.

"Yes, Ma'am, I'm sure I want to go to college if I can. But mom, what made you bring it up? I've never mentioned it to you."

The issue was settled, the tension broken. With her expression and voice now relaxed, she cheerfully replied, "Well, I've noticed you've been spending more time studying, and you've been making honor roll grades. Besides, a little birdie told me."

"OK, Mom, who's the little birdie?" Charlie chided, a little irritated at her coy answer.

"Well, if you must know, it was Mrs. Compton."

"Mrs. Compton? My eighth grade English teacher? I haven't seen or talked to her in over three years except to say hello," said Charlie.

Chris continued, "Well, you know she's a customer at the station. She was in today for gas and told me. She said she and some other teachers were talking about you, how you've turned around. She said Mrs. Wardlaw asked you about college, and you said you wanted to go, but that we couldn't afford it. She said Mrs. Wardlaw, Miss Earnest, Mrs. Brinson and she herself all thought you should go to college."

Charlie was surprised and flattered. He remembered that all of those teachers had taken a particular interest in him and encouraged him, telling him he was smart enough to do anything he wanted, but he never believed them.

Charlie was still processing what he had just heard when Chris continued, "I know Mrs. Compton, but who are those other teachers? I don't know them."

Charlie explained. "Miss Earnest was my sophomore World History teacher, and I have her for Government this year. Remember, she's the one who calls me 'Bonnie Prince Charlie'? Mrs. Brinson was my American History teacher last year, and Mrs. Wardlaw is the one who transferred me to her AP Senior English class. She took me to the school office and showed me my aptitude scores. She told me I was smart enough that I ought to go to college."

Chris said, "Well, son, they all think a lot of you and hope you will go. And I know you can do it. We've got to get busy if you're going to college. So, let's go eat. Then you can finish your homework."

"One more thing mom, you said you prayed for Gene and me?"

"Oh, son, I have prayed for you and Gene almost every night since you were born. I still do, and I guess I always will. You boys will never stop being my babies."

Chris had opened up to him more than ever before, and Charlie saw a part of his mother he had not known. "I never knew any of that, Mom." Not wanting to miss this opportunity to get answers he'd long wondered about, he continued. "While we're talking Mom, can I ask you how come you and Dad divorced?"

For the next hour, Chris explained everything and answered all his questions as honestly as she could. She explained that she never said anything about their dad's shortcomings, because she didn't want he and Gene to grow up with a bad impression of him.

Charlie was accepted at Virginia Tech in the Corps of Cadets. The cost was financed with loans that Chris signed for, scholarships based on financial need, plus what Chris and he could contribute from money they earned, but mostly what she earned.

In his early days at college, when doing university-level work was the hardest, Charlie remembered that moment, all that Chris had said, and all that he came to understand and appreciate about her. It was that which picked him up when he felt down, kept him going when he thought he could not, and propelled him to excel when he thought he would be lucky just to make passing grades.

CHAPTER 39

A FATEFUL DECISION

A real estate agent walked into the station one day in 1957 and asked to speak to the owner. Dick Mahle and Chris came out and met with him. He said he represented a bank that was looking for property for a new branch, and that they were interested in the station property. Over the next few days Mahle thought about it and talked it over, and over, and over with Chris.

Though she was a partner in the business, he alone owned the building and land. Mahle was definitely interested. The final take-it-or-leave-it deal was more than he thought it was worth, and he wanted to sell. He figured they could go down the street a ways and find another lot on Lakeside Avenue, build a new building, mortgage it and pocket most of the cash from the sale.

Chris was strongly against it. She believed the corner location at that busy intersection was worth a lot more. She argued that a significant percentage of customers came to the station mainly because of its convenient location. She was convinced that those customers would not likely follow the business to a new location in the middle of a block further down the street.

Mahle, as sole owner of the land and building, got what he wanted. It turned out Chris was right. The new location did not attract the traffic of the corner location. In fact, at one time, the new station was carrying a big mortgage payment, business was slow and they used up its bank line of credit. They needed $10,000 to make payroll and pay late bills. Mahle could not borrow any more money and was at his wits end.

Chris, who was not on the note or mortgage for the new place, was able to borrow on her signature alone the $10,000 from her bank. When she presented Mahle the check, he was amazed and happily took the money. She never asked him to sign a promissory note for the money, and he never offered. *After all,* she told herself, *we are partners.*

From there, the business of the station was temporarily moved to a rented gas station next to a small shopping center near Hilliard Road and Lakeside Avenue. It was pretty enough and had ample driveway and parking space, but it had fewer repair bays. Still, they were able to make do until the new building was built closer to the corner of Lakeside and Dumbarton.

While moving the business had its downside, for Chris, there was one important upside. One day an old gentleman pulled his car into the station. Chris thought he looked familiar but could not place him. She went out to help him. It turned out that he worked for the county. He said his name was Buckley.

The name was distantly familiar, not as a brand of automobile, but the name of a person she once knew. Fond memories began to effervesce. A memory bubbled to the surface and popped. In that instant, Chris remembered him. "I know who you are. My dad was Harry Morris. You and he worked together at the railroad before the Depression. You knew me as Christine when I was a little girl," she said enthusiastically.

He looked her over as she spoke. Recognition soon bloomed in his eyes. They talked about all they had experienced since he and Harry had been laid off by the railroad back in 1930. He had been widowed for some years, lived alone, and his children, all grown and married, were busy with their own families.

Mr. Buckley worked for Henrico County and had an encyclo-
pedic knowledge of the locations of all county's underground
utility systems. He was well beyond the age of retirement, but he
was indispensable to the county. Chris took him under her wing,
and from then until he died, she took care of him, getting him to
and from the doctor and dentist, seeing that he ate properly, that
his house was cleaned, that he bathed regularly and brushed his
teeth. He was a robust old gentleman and actually maintained a
small vegetable garden on his property, located on Hungary Road,
which at that time was in the country. Old Mr. Buckley was very
special to Chris because he was a direct link to her dad, whom she
had adored and missed.

Gene and Charlie, especially Charlie, took to Mr. Buckley, who
entertained them with his sage quips and stories about the "old
days." Mr. Buckley's father had served in General Lee's army during the Civil War and survived right through to the surrender at
Appomattox Courthouse.

He showed the boys a Civil War musket that had been his
father's and other Confederate military gear, such as a wooden
canteen and a powder horn, both of which he eventually gave to
Charlie as payment for outside chores he had done for the old gentleman. Charlie treasured both the canteen and the powder horn.

When Mr. Buckley became too feeble to take care of himself,
his children put him in a nursing home. Chris offered to continue
to take care of him, but they felt that she had gone out of her way
to help him for a long time, and she had her own health to be
concerned about. She said she didn't think he would last long in
a nursing home, but they insisted. Just as Chris had warned, Mr.
Buckley soon died. Chris believed his arrival at the station that
day was no mere coincidence.

CHAPTER 40

THE SLEEPER

One morning in December, 1961, Chris went out to her car to run an errand before work. As she walked up to it, she saw a sleeping boy curled up in a fetal position on the back seat. She made him out to be about 14 years old. He looked clean-cut enough. He reminded her a little of her own boys when they were that age, or maybe she wished he did.

She opened her car door, and the sleeping boy woke with a start. "What are you doing here?" she asked her tone one of curiosity tinged with wariness.

"I . . . I'm sorry, Ma'am. I'll go now," the boy said as he hurriedly slid toward the door across the leather seat of Chris's Lincoln.

Chris positioned herself in the door opening and firmly grasped the door with one hand and the door frame in the other. "Not so fast son." She wasn't sure whether to call the police, chase him away with a stern warning or something else. She opted to investigate further. She quickly looked him over. He was clean cut, had nice, clean though wrinkled clothes, a head of thick, dark brown hair that had been recently cut, a pleasant face, brown eyes and clean complexion, except for a bruise on one cheek.

What's your name?" Again, her tone was one of curiosity.

"Gary," he said sheepishly.

"Gary who?" she asked.

"Swain, Gary Swain."

"Where do you live, it must be near here?" she asked.

"Parkside Avenue" That was only four blocks away.

"With your parents?" Chris continued.

"Yes, Ma'am."

"Well why aren't you at home in bed?"

He turned his eyes away and looked down. In a weak voice, he answered, "I can't go home. My dad kicked me out of the house."

"Come on Gary, let's go inside where it's warm. I'll fix you some breakfast, and we can talk."

He followed Chris into her house and was soon wolfing down scrambled eggs, toast, bacon and hash brown potatoes. Chris guessed he had not had dinner the night before, so she whipped up a double portion of everything and poured a tall glass of cold milk. While Gary ate, Chris learned that his dad, in drunken anger, had punched him and bodily threw him out of the house, telling him he was stupid, no good, and not to come back - all for a typical 14-year-old's minor failing. It seems that sort of thing had become a regular part of Gary's life at home. His mother was too frightened to do anything to protect the boy.

When she had learned enough, Chris announced her decision. "Gary, I'm not going to call the police on you, but I do want you to call your mother, tell her where you are and that you are alright. The phone is right over there," she said, nodding toward the black table-top telephone.

Gary dialed his home number and waited as it rang. "Mom? It's me. I'm OK. Mom, don't cry, it's alright, I'm OK. It didn't hurt that much. I'm over on Kent Street. I spent the night in a car, and this morning a really nice lady fixed me breakfast. I'm at her house now. It was her car that I slept in . . . Uh, yes, Ma'am. Wait a second."

Gary turned to Chris. "My mom wants to talk to you." He handed her the phone.

"Hello, this is Chris Payne . . . It's nice to meet you too Mrs. Swain . . . Ok then, Mary it is. It's nice to meet you Mary." Gary's mother thanked her, apologized and offered to pay her. Chris assured her no apology or payment was needed and said she was glad to help her boy.

Within a few minutes, Chris and Gary were sitting in his mother's living room. His father was at work. Gary and his mother explained the whole background of his dad's drinking and the violence that always went with it. Mary said she didn't know what to do, that he was a good man and she loved him, but he just had this problem; that she couldn't leave him even if she wanted to because she had nowhere else to go, and she had never held a job outside the home, so she couldn't support herself.

Chris understood Mary's story all too well. As the woman talked, Chris was thinking she could have been in Mary's shoes if she had not had the courage to leave Emmett. Chris suggested that Mary talk to Child Protective Services and explained about something called a "peace bond." In a few days, Gary was back at home, his father was under a peace bond and had voluntarily entered alcohol treatment. Even so, Gary continued to make his way to Chris's house when she was home and to the station when she was at work.

When Charlie came home from college for Christmas that year, he hitched a ride with a classmate named Butch. He was about five foot five and pudgy. Butch and Charlie, still wearing their Virginia Tech cadet uniforms, pulled up in front of the house, got out and headed for the front door. Suddenly, the door flew open and Chris ran out, leaped off the porch, nearly tackled Charlie, swept him up in her arms, suitcase and all, and swung him around in a full circle, flinging his cadet hat off his head. "Oh, son!" she exclaimed, "I'm so glad you're home!"

Butch, who was right behind Charlie, stopped in his tracks. His eyes popped out and his jaw dropped in awe of Chris. After all, Charlie weighed 190 lbs and was 6 foot1, yet Chris was swinging him around as if he were a four year old. The three went inside and Butch used the bathroom, then left for his own home.

As Charlie unpacked and changed out of his cadet uniform, Chris told him about Gary and asked him to spend some time with him. She later introduced them, and they hit it off right away. Gary became a regular companion of Charlie's for the Christmas break. Later, when Charlie returned home from college for summer break, Gary occasionally went along with Charlie and his girlfriend, Brenda Bass, on outings, such as to a rock-and-roll concert or to play miniature golf or to just ride around. Charlie's girlfriend didn't mind, and the three of them had fun together. Often, just Charlie and Gary got together for a guys-only outing.

Chris and Charlie both urged Gary not to accept his father's words, things like being stupid and worthless, to remember that he is the one who gets to decide how well or badly he does in life, and that he gets to decide what he wants to do. Charlie urged him to set high goals for himself and pursue them with total determination. Having the friendship and advice seemed to help Gary's feelings about himself and his father. When Charlie was away at Tech, Chris spent time with Gary, continuing to give him encouragement and approval. He became attached to her as if she were his favorite aunt. That went on for a year or more.

CHAPTER 41

ICE AND SNOW

About January or February, 1964, Chris's 45th year, a snowfall blanketed Richmond. As usually happens, the snow turned to ice wherever car tires packed it down. Such was the case on the concrete apron in front of the station. At work one day, a lady customer pulled up to the pumps and an employee went out to serve her. Chris recognized her from the office and went out to greet her. When she stepped off the curb both feet slipped on the ice and she fell hard on the base of her spine. She got back up immediately, ignored the lingering pain, and went out to see the customer.

As the days rolled by, the pain persisted and gradually worsened. Mahle concluded it was a "sprained sacroiliac joint." His idea was that it would go away by itself, and all Chris had to do was carry on and take something for the pain if she needed it. Chris went along with his assessment. True to her nature, she did not let a little discomfort get her down. She just persevered and went right on working, taking aspirin for pain as needed.

On another snowy, bitter cold night, Chris was at home with Charlie, who was on Christmas break from college. They had just finished a dinner of Chinese takeout and were talking about his courses that semester. Their conversation was interrupted by sudden loud knocking at the door and the sound of it opening. "Hello. Chris?" Addie Johnson called out.

"Come on in," Chris replied, always happy to get a surprise visit from her friend.

Moments later, Addie, Betty and Helen came into the kitchen.

Chris was pleasantly excited to see the girls. Having never had the daughter she wanted, Chris had taken to Addie's as if they were her own. "Oh, hi girls," she said, "What are you doing out on a night like this?"

Helen answered, "We want to build a snowman in your yard, and we want you to help us. Chris had had the traditional closing-time shot of bourbon with the boys at the station, followed at home by a pain pill chased by a couple more bourbon shots. Her constant pain was masked, noticeably elevating her mood. The girl's excitement infected Chris. "Want to?" she asked.

"Does that mean we can do it and you'll help?" asked Betty.

"Yes," replied Chris, "What about you, Addie? Are you going to join us?"

"No, I don't think so," Addie said. "My arthritis is acting up with this change in the weather and all. I think I'll stay inside, but you go on ahead, Chris, and I'll watch from the window."

Helen spoke up. "What about you Charlie? Are you coming'?"

Charlie was not so enthusiastic. He said, "Mom, I don't think you should be going out in this weather to build a snowman. Your back is giving you a lot of pain, and you know if you do it you'll pay dearly tomorrow.

"Aw, Charlie, I'm not worried about that," she said with a dismissive waive of the hand. "Come on and help us."

'No, Mom, I don't want to do it if you're going to be out there in it. I'm afraid you'll make your back worse. But I'll do it with Helen and Betty, and you can watch from the window with Mrs. Johnson."

"That's my worry. Come on, girls, let's go," said Chris, as she stood up and headed out of the kitchen. Stubborn as she was, Chris was not going to listen to him. Charlie and Chris both knew she would be in a lot of pain later after the alcohol and pain pills wore off.

He was about to try one last time, more insistently, when Addie discretely took Charlie's arm. Leaned slightly toward his ear she whispered, "It's OK. Let her have her fun with the girls."

Charlie turned and looked sideways at Addie. She made eye contact and nodded in silence. It all became clear to him. It had been the girls' idea to build a snowman and Addie's idea to come to Chris's house and get Chris to join in.

Addie was a loyal friend to Chris, and she knew her back was giving her a fit. She also knew that Chris building a snowman with Betty and Helen would in some way let Chris recapture the care-free adolescence which the vagaries of life had mostly denied to her. She wanted Chris to have the memory of that night, of playing in the snow with Betty and Helen. Charlie then understood and kept his silence.

Charlie and Addie remained in the house, watching from a living room window while Chris, Betty and Helen spent a good hour in bitter-cold weather, building a dandy, five-foot- tall roly-poly snowman. They set about decorating it whimsically while continuing to intermittently throw snowballs at each other and shove handfuls of snow down each other's collars.

Charlie, who understood her well, could tell that it was a special moment for Chris – a chance to pretend to be a mom to two daughters, joining them in a youthful frolic. Maybe it also reminded her of her childhood days playing in the snow with Edythe and Evelyn. Whatever was going through her mind, she had a high time in more ways than one.

That romp in the snow took its toll just as Charlie expected. Chris's back was in agony and she was sore all over for the next several days. She also had a touch of laryngitis to boot. Even so, the joy of that occasion could be seen in her face every time she related the story of the adventure. To her, the playtime with "her" girls was worth the pain she had to know would follow.

CHAPTER 42
THE FENCE POST

I t was autumn, 1964, the weather dry and warm, the nights mild. Like so many other nights before, Chris came home from work, ate a simple dinner, watched a little TV and went to bed to read a few chapters in the paperback mystery novel she had started two nights before. It was the latest of perhaps a few hundred mystery and romance novels that she had read over the years.

A half hour later, she turned off her nightstand light, said her nightly prayers and turned onto her side to ease the ever-present back pain. A soothing current of cool night air slipped through the screen covering her open bedroom window. She pulled the sheet a little more snugly around her shoulders and neck, and drifted off to sleep. It was about 12:00 midnight.

A faint noise, not a cricket, not a frog nor a distant car horn, tickled her consciousness. Moments later another faint sound rippled her slumber. She began to stir just a little. Then another and she was suddenly awake and on alert. She listened without moving a muscle. An almost inaudible sound reached her ear from outside her bedroom window.

She rolled her head just enough that both ears could tune in. There it was again, definitely, a sound from outside right at her window; the sound of something or someone quietly tampering with the frame of the screen. She turned her eyes toward the window without moving her head. There, in the faint light of a streetlamp on the next street over, she could see the silhouette of a man from shoulders up framed by the open window.

Chris propelled herself out of bed and shouted, "Who's there?"

Whoever it was vanished in a fraction of a second. She called the police, who came roaring up the street with emergency lights flashing and siren screaming. When the policemen arrived and looked around, surprise, surprise, they found no prowler, just man-sized footprints in the flower bed. They said they would write a report, but, without evidence of who it was, there was nothing more they could do.

Chris had heard that one before in her last house. Her suggestion that the police lay off the lights and sirens was brushed off. They acted as if the whole thing were just a figment of her imagination. What's that old saying? "Stupid is when you repeatedly do the same thing in the same way expecting a different result."

Figuring that she couldn't depend on the police for effective help, Chris decided she would have to protect herself . . . again. She began the habit of putting her pistol on the nightstand, safety off. She also didn't allow herself to sleep as soundly. The very next moonless night, one month later, the weather was still warm, Chris still had her windows open, and the shadowy prowler came again to visit.

When she heard faint sounds in the backyard, she was instantly and fully awake. She lay still, waiting, watching. Sure enough, she saw the dark silhouette of a man quietly approaching the outside window sill.

She girded herself for the back pain she knew was coming, and slowly, silently, rolled herself out of bed and onto her knees. She eased her gun off the nightstand, crawled from bedroom to hallway, where she rose to her bare feet and made her way to the back door, which was about 15 feet from her bedroom window.

Wearing just her pajamas, Chris, ever so quietly released the latch. She paused, readied her pistol, making sure the safety was off, took a deep breath, clenched her teeth against the rising back pain, then yanked the door open and jumped out onto the porch with a loud clatter. The prowler, standing 15 feet away at her bedroom window, jumped like a startled rabbit. He took off for the back fence as if the devil himself was nipping at his backside. Chris pointed her pistol and fired at him in rapid succession: Bang! Bang! She paused, aimed carefully, and fired again just as the man was in mid-air, pole vaulting on a fence post.

The prowler, dressed in dark clothes, pale faced, with black hair, disappeared into the night. Chris phoned the police, put on her robe and waited. Officer Sweeney was on duty and received the dispatcher's call. He came and listened as Chris told him what had happened. Outside he found fresh, man-sized footprints in the flower bed below Chris's window, just as before.

With the bright lights on the roof of the patrol car still flashing, Officer Sweeny scolded Chris for shooting at the prowler, reminded her that it was illegal to discharge a firearm in a populated area of the county, that if she had hit him she would be charged, and blah, blah, blah.

With Chris standing nearby, clad in robe and slippers but not cuffed, Sweeny, oozing confidence, called in on his car radio: "Car 203 to Dis'patch."

Dispatcher: "Go ahead 203."

Sweeny: "Dis'patch, I got a situation here. I need to talk to the lieutenant?"

Dispatcher: "Hold while I get him, 203."

In surrounding houses, lights began coming on, people were peeking out of their windows and a group of neighbors were gathering in the street but keeping a discreet distance. They knew Chris and were there out of concern for her. Chris nodded and smiled at them and some of the ladies smiled back. The police radio crackled on: "Headquarters to 203: Sweeny, this is Lt. Samuels. What's your situation?"

Sweeny: "Lieutenant, Sir, I'm on Kent Street, in Lakeside, on the call from the lady about a prowler. I found fresh-looking footprints in the flower bed below her bedroom window. The window was open, and she says she saw a man looking in there and doing something with the screen. She snuck out her back door with a pistol and surprised him. He ran, and she shot at him. There are three empty chambers and the gun smells like it's just been fired. She says she missed. I found a bullet stuck in a fence post at the rear of her yard where she says the prowler jumped the fence. Should I bring her in now or tell her to turn herself in tomorrow morning?"

Lieutenant Samuels: "Bring her in, for what?"

Sweeny: "Well, for attempting to shoot the man, discharging a firearm in a populated area and disturbing the peace?"

Lieutenant Samuels: "For Pete sake, Sweeny, I know that lady. She was defending herself and her home from a prowler whose intentions were God-knows-what. If a man shows up at the hospital tonight or tomorrow with a bullet in his backside, I'll think about it. But right now I'm classifying it as an attempted felony breaking-and-entering, self-defense on her part, with no harm done by her. Let her go back to bed, and you get back on the street."

Officer Sweeny: "Let her go, Sir?"

Lieutenant Samuels: "Yes, let her go. Oh, and one more thing, how far is it from where she fired the gun to the fence post with the bullet in it?"

Officer Sweeny: "It looks to be about 75 or 80 feet, Sir."

Lt. Samuels: "Tell her I said good shoot'n' but next time to hold her fire 'til the guy is crawling in her window."

CHAPTER 43

THE PIPER COLLECTS

The fall on the ice that wintery night at the station and Chris's continuing pain was getting progressively worse. Chris eventually developed weakness and electrical sensations down one leg. Occasionally it would just collapse. She finally went to Dr. Le Fon. He referred her to a spine specialist. The diagnosis was two herniated discs in her lower spine. As time went by without treatment, the damaged discs had begun to pinch nerve branches, causing the electric sensations and the radiating pain, both of which she had endured far too long before getting medical help.

Spine surgery was done in the summer of 1964. The discs were removed and the three vertebrae involved were fused together into one solid bone, with grafts from her hip. This limited the flexibility of her spine and stopped the nerve damage from getting worse. It did not stop or even improve the pain she already lived with, and it added a new chronic pain in her hip. Even so, Chris continued to work with dogged determination.

The smoking habit that she'd taken up early in her career at the station gradually grew to more than two packs a day. Also, the practice of having a shot of bourbon every night at closing time went on for years even after she became a partner and Mahle started going home at 5:00 p.m.

None of the prescription pain medicine actually eased her pain, but a little whiskey and the pain medicine together really took it down to a tolerable level. Chris's alcohol use grew until she was addicted. It got so bad that she was at least a little high almost all the time – enough that her sons could tell, and so could customers at the station. Dick Mahle eventually terminated her job. That was just as well, because the simple truth is that even if she had not become an alcoholic, she should not have been on her feet moving around, bending and lifting.

Chris's problems didn't end there. According to her, Mahle said she was not real partner in the business but only a 10% profit partner, an arrangement which he was free to cancel at any time. According to her, he never repaid the $10,000 loan that Chris had made to him. Though she was deeply hurt, she did nothing to pursue what she felt were legitimate claims. She balanced her hurt feelings and loss of the money against her gratitude to Mahle for giving her a chance, teaching her, paying for her advance school training, treating her as an equal, and for being understanding and flexible about her need to take care of her boys.

She did apply for Worker's Comp disability and was awarded all of her medical expenses and the maximum amount of disability income that was allowable, two-thirds of her base pay for 500 weeks. At that time, the Social Security's disability benefit was still in its infancy and only paid for rehabilitation expenses for injured workers over age 50, but it paid no living expenses. At the time, Chris was only 45 years old. The result was that she did not qualify for SSDI. As for the station's business, and the fellow employees and customers, all of whom she loved, once Chris was gone, nothing was the same.

CHAPTER 44

CRABS AND CROW

Among her recreational passions, Chris also loved to go fishing and crabbing. Living in Richmond, she didn't often get to do those things, but when she got the chance she jumped on it. In 1973, Chris made one of her visits to Virginia Beach to see Charlie, his wife Carolyn and their kids. It was summer, so Chris and Carolyn went to the 14th Street Pier and crabbed for most of the day. Meanwhile, Charlie, by then called "Chuck", was putting in a long day at his law office in the Virginia National Bank building in Norfolk.

Charlie arrived home, tired and thirsty, to find tubs and tubs of blue crabs on ice, which the two of them were cooking, one large pot at a time. There were so many crabs that Charlie thought for sure there wouldn't be enough left to repopulate the species. He asked, "What on earth do you plan to do with all those?"

Chris, in a matter-of-fact and slightly indignant tone, replied "We're going to cook them, pick them and freeze them in pint containers. I think we'll have enough to fill your freezer and mine." Anticipating his next question, she added, "I'll buy some dry ice for the drive back to Richmond."

Incredulous at the very thought of accomplishing that herculean feat, Charlie stated with supreme confidence, "You will never get all those crabs picked. Why on earth did you keep on catching them when you had to know you had more than you could handle?"

That's when Chris learned that she and Carolyn shared the same irresistible compulsion to do the impossible. Charlie's goose was cooked. By the end of the next day every one of those crabs had been cooked, picked clean, the meat packed in individual pint-sized plastic freezer containers, the kitchen cleaned up and deodorized, and all the shells double-bagged and put out in the trash can for pick up. If Charlie had not seen it with his own eyes, he would have thought the whole thing was a made-up story.

Chris, Charlie and Carolyn ate their fill of crab while Chris was staying with them that week. Carolyn also gave some away to her family and friends. Chris took a bunch of pints home with her, and even after that, there were still a dozen or more pints in Carolyn's freezer. For many months after that, Charlie ate delicious crab cakes, crab scampi, crab salad, crab in rice, and flounder stuffed with crab, each topped with a big helping of crow.

CHAPTER 45

A JOURNEY'S END

In early 1974, Ruth Morris became too feeble to live alone. Chris had her come live with her, even though Chris herself by that time had serious back problems as well as growing alcoholism. She fed, bathed and dressed Ruth, washed and dried her thin hair, brushed it out, plaited it and coiled it into Ruth's signature crown, just as Ruth had done for many, many years. Chris took her to her doctors and nursed her along until Ruth could no longer stand up on her own and was clearly sinking. Chris could not lift her. On doctor's orders, she reluctantly put her mother, Ruth, in a nursing home.

About a month later, Chris called Charlie at his home in Virginia Beach. Through her tears she said "Mother" was bad off. She was in a coma and the doctors wanted to stop life support. They said there was no real hope for her to get better.

She explained that Henry and Perk could not bring themselves to give the order and said she should do whatever she thought was best. Then, Chris, the stalwart pillar of strength and courage, began to cry profusely and said, "But I can't do it, I just can't. Will you call the doctor and give the order?"

Charlie said, "I'll do it if she is really that close to death, but I need to see Granny and talk to the doctors myself."

The next day, Charlie cancelled his appointments and drove to Richmond, where he and Chris met the doctors at the nursing home. They confirmed the situation and reported that Ruth was not likely to come out of the coma. Even if she did it would only be a short waking spell, and that there was no need for her to continue to suffer. Chris and Charlie then went into the room to see Ruth. She was unconscious. Softly, Chris said, "Mother, are you awake?"

"She probably can't respond to you," the doctor said.

"Mother, it's Chris. Wake up now," Chris continued. Still no response. Chris added, "Mother, Charlie is here to see you,"

"Hi Granny, it's Charlie," he said in a soft, cheerful voice.

Ruth stirred, then her tired old eyes opened a little and she slowly looked around the room until she saw Chris and Charlie standing on either side of her bed. She had a few sweet moments with them, during which Chris and Charlie held her hands. They talked about her condition and mentioned going home and seeing Harry, Evelyn and Edythe. Ruth's eyes became misty. Charlie told her what the doctors had said, then lovingly asked, "Granny, do you want to go?"

Ruth looked at him and him at her. Ruth's eyes, filling with tears, were saying yes, she was ready to go, but she would miss each one of her family she leaves behind. Chris kissed her forehead and told her she loved her. Charlie squeezed her hand, kissed her forehead and whispered, "I love you, Granny. We'll be with you again one day"

Charlie struggled mightily to maintain composure. Finally, he leaned down close to his grandmother's face. Ruth's eyes met his, and he whispered, "Goodbye, Granny."

Ruth looked deep into Charlie's eyes, her expression saying she understood this was final. Then she closed her eyes and peacefully slipped back into the coma. Chris cried quietly as she left the room. Charlie remained at Ruth's bedside. When Chris was out of the room, Doctor Le Fon and a nurse entered. Charlie gave the go-ahead to the doctor, who in turn nodded to the nurse. The life support machines were turned off. In a few short hours, Ruth Perkins Morris graduated to heaven. It was August 19, 1974. She was 87 years of age. Her funeral was attended by all of her children and grandchildren, and perhaps one or more of the few surviving friends that were still alive and well enough to get there. Ruth's many grand children, especially the younger ones, were heartbroken.

CHAPTER 46

ONE MORE APPLE PIE

At age 57, in 1976, Chris was diagnosed with cancer of the mouth, traceable to the combined effects of smoking and drinking. It is now known that the risk of cancer is greatly increased when regular use of tobacco and alcohol are combined.

After the cancer surgery and for the rest of her life, Chris had to use a blender to turn her food into something like a milkshake, which she had to inject directly into her stomach through a tube permanently protruding through her side.

The benefits of the treatment were that she was cured of cancer and never again touched tobacco or whisky. She did, however, use prescription painkillers for her continuing back and hip pain, and those were themselves addictive. When it looked like they were getting the best of her, she would go to the doctor for a detoxification.

Though afflicted by permanent back injury and cancer, Chris continued to live her life as fully as she could for 12 more years after her cancer treatment. She refused to move in with either Gene or Charlie, or into a convalescent center. As she put it, "those places are for old people." She continued to own and drive a car, spent time with her grandchildren, and became friends with the other people in her apartment building. She regularly cooked meals and baked pies and cakes for her neighbor friends, though she couldn't eat what she cooked. When she wasn't taking care of others, Chris continued her life-long enjoyment of mystery novels, though that was gradually replaced by reading her Bible, inspirational books and magazines.

In 1987, Chris's blood chemistry started going way out of balance. The doctors never found a cause for it. She was admitted to the hospital through the emergency room and listed Gene's phone number as the number to call in the worst case. They treated the symptoms, she rallied, got better overnight and was sent home, where she did well for a time.

That happened several times. During these episodes in the hospital, when she rallied, Chris would be up and on her feet, dropping in to see other patients, cheering them up and encouraging them. The nurses soon began telling her of patients who had no family or friends. Chris would be sure to drop by see them as long as she was still an in-patient herself.

One day at home her blood pressure suddenly dropped so low that she fainted. In the hospital she was listed as critical. After hours of tests and treatments, the doctors called Gene and advised that she was close to death and would pass within the next 24 hours. He, in turn, notified Charlie. They girded for the worst.

The next day, Gene's phone rang. "Hello?" he answered.

"Hi son. I'm ready to go home now. Can you come pick me up?" Chris asked, though her usual cheeriness seemed less than genuine. Her blood chemistry and blood pressure had inexplicably returned to normal.

One day soon after that, Chris decided to bake a pie for a lady friend who lived upstairs, just above her apartment. When asked why she did it, Chris answered, "Because she's had a rough time with her health lately, I thought a homemade pie would cheer her up. She likes my pies."

Two days later, Chris was taken yet again to the hospital and listed in critical condition. Again, it was her blood pressure bottoming out. The doctors said she would likely not survive the attack, but yet again she did. Wide awake and in a cheerful mood, she leaned over, picked up the phone and dialed. Before Gene answered, her eyes closed and her head fell to the pillow. Her vital signs monitor flat-lined. She had already signed a "Do Not Resuscitate" order, so no effort was made to revive her. In 18 more days she would have celebrated her 70th birthday. That day, October 1, 1989, Chris went to join her mom, dad, Edythe and Evelyn.

Chris's funeral at Hatcher Memorial was simple and without frills, as she wanted it. In attendance were family members, children and daughters-in-law, most of her grandchildren, nieces and nephews, some old friends who loved her like family, and some newer friends, including the lady for whom she had baked her last pie.

Chris is buried at Forest Land Cemetery, in Ashland, VA, in a plot that Gene and his wife, Pattie, bought to accommodate both Chris and themselves. Among Chris's many friends and admirers were housewives, school teachers, business owners, lawyers, a Virginia Supreme Court Justice, Circuit Court Judges, pastors, a host of doctors, the staff and volunteers at the Red Cross office in Lakeside, and many people in the automobile industry, from dealership owners to service managers and shop mechanics. As of this writing there are still some, now getting old, who remember Chris and speak of her with fondness and admiration.

CHAPTER 47

A TRAIL WELL MARKED

Major Holcomb

In late November, 1965, US Army paratrooper, 1st Lieutenant Charlie Payne, was sent to Vietnam and assigned to the 1st Brigade of the legendary 101st Airborne Division. When he arrived at brigade headquarters to report for duty, he found that it was housed in one of the several large, general-purpose, olive green tents arranged in an orderly grid. He was escorted by a Master Sergeant to a tent marked by a wooden sign saying, "Admin Section." Most of the side curtains of the tent were rolled up due to the suffocating heat. There was no floor, just the ground, which was mostly sand. At one end of the tent was a platform fabricated from 105mm howitzer ammunition boxes. On the platform was an olive-green, portable field desk. Behind the desk sat a youthful looking major dressed in jungle fatigues and tropical combat boots. He was studiously reading a file that lay opened on his desk.

The Master Sergeant approached and said, "Major Holcomb, sir."

The major looked up. "This is Lieutenant Payne. He and his team just arrived. They are here to report for duty."

The major glanced at Charlie then cut his eyes to the sergeant. "Very well, Sergeant. Thanks. I'll take it from here."

The sergeant pivoted and walked away. Charlie stepped up to the desk and announced, "Lieutenant Payne reporting for duty, Sir." No salutes were exchanged. In a tactical situation salutes help the enemy identify the officers who then become sought after targets.

The major looked at Charlie and said, "Welcome aboard Lieutenant." He then looked down at the thick yellow envelope in Charlie's left hand. Charlie extended the envelope, and the major took it.

"I'm Major Holcomb, Assistant Brigade Admin Officer. Have a seat, lieutenant" he said, pointing down to Charlie's immediate right. "Let's have a look at these personnel records."

Charlie looked down and saw a 105mm Howitzer ammo crate sitting up on end next to his right knee. He removed his head gear and sat on it. The major untied the string that held the envelope's flap closed, drew out the files inside, one for each member of the team, chose Charlie's personnel file and began looking through it. He quickly scanned several pages, stopping to read a few pertinent details, muttering as he read: "Selected for special training. Deployed with 82nd Airborne to Dominican Republic, detailed to 18th Airborne Corps HQ for special assignment." He continued to read in silence for a few moments.

Suddenly looking up, the Major said, "I see you were commissioned at Virginia Tech in '62. So, you're a Hokie?"

"Yes, Sir," replied Charlie, a bit surprised.

"So am I." The major quickly flipped to a different place in the 201 file. "It says here your home of record is Richmond, Virginia."

"Yes Sir."

The major then read the name in the blank labeled "Next of Kin." Surprise washed over his face: "Chris Payne is your next of kin?" he blurted.

"Yes Sir. She is my mother," replied Charlie, his face lit up.

"Well, hell, Lieutenant," Major Holcomb gushed, "I grew up in Lakeside. My father owned a business, "Holcomb Contract Cleaning." He had a crew that cleaned offices at night. We were regular customers at your mother's station. I saw her many times when I worked part-time for my dad during high school. In fact, I knew you and your brother. Gene's his name, right?"

"Yes it is," replied Charlie, old memories flooding back. "Now that you mention it, I remember seeing you a couple of times with your father when he stopped at the station. You look a little older, but I definitely remember seeing you. The truck your father drove was green, with the name of his business painted on the side, right?"

"Yes, he had several trucks, all green, and you must have seen me. I was in there regularly for awhile, filling up a company truck." the major continued. He paused, as if reflecting on old memories, shaking his head from side to side and grinning. He leaned over the portable field desk. "Charlie," he said, in a quiet, deliberate voice, "Your mother is something special! She is a lady and was a real beauty when she was younger. I always looked forward to going to the station, hoping I'd get to see her. What amazed me about her was that she could fix anything - I mean *anything* - that had a motor and ran on wheels, and she could do it better than most anybody. But I guess you know all that."

The major leaned even closer, his expression becoming serious, "Lieutenant, I want you to know that I have always had the greatest respect and admiration for your mother. She is one of a kind. My father had a habit of not paying his bills. He ran up a big bill at the station, and when she pressed him, he jerked her around like he did everybody else he owed money to. It was something I wasn't very proud of. Most people would settle for a partial payment rather than fight him. But your mother took him to court and got a judgment, and she didn't even hire a lawyer. With that hanging over his head, my dad paid up, with interest. He met his match with your mother, and I was glad for her."

Charlie, flattered and proud, thanked him warmly. The major then put his army persona back on and got back to business, but a whole different flavor was added to the meeting. He went out of his way to help Charlie learn the many little things that junior-grade officers arriving in Vietnam usually learned as they go. He greased the skids, so to speak, putting in a good word for Charlie with the brigade commander and staff. Major Holcomb was soon re-assigned back to the States. Charlie never saw him again, but he was grateful for what the major had said about Chris and for his help, which was nothing less than a display of his regard for her.

Gary Swain

In 1972, young Gary Swain, all grown up, drove from his home in North Carolina and showed up in Virginia Beach at Charlie's home. There, in Charlie's kitchen, Gary declined an offer of a cold beer, saying that after seeing what it did to his dad, he never drank.

Over a cup of coffee, Gary told Charlie he had finished high school, left home for North Carolina, was married, had two children and owned a wonderful suburban home in a solid upper-middle class neighborhood in the Raleigh-Durham area. He said he had started at minimum wage in a franchise business and was now the general manager of a chain of stores.

He said he was headed to Richmond to see his parents, and to see Chris to tell her how much she had meant to him. He said his father gave up drinking, joined his wife in an active church life and that they were happy. He also had reconciled with Gary, and they got along well.

Charlie Jones

Lakeside Community Barbershop opened one Saturday morning in 1995, just as the first customer of the day walked in. Charlie Jones, the proprietor, had been cutting hair in that location for decades. He knew all of his customers and he knew the history of Lakeside and many of its people going back to the 1940s. He also knew that the nice-looking young man with an overgrown crew cut who walked into his shop that morning was new to the shop and to Lakeside.

"Morning!" said Charlie Jones.

"Good morning!" answered the young man, "Are you open?"

"I sure am. You're my first customer today," he replied, motioning the customer to the big, hydraulic barber chair.

"Great," replied the young fellow, proceeding to climb into it.

Jones quickly fastened the drape around his neck. Picking up his comb and electric shears, he asked, "You want the same cut you have now, just shorter?"

"Yeah, that's good," replied the customer.

Jones began combing and shearing. "Do you live in Lakeside?"

"Yes, Sir," the customer answered, "My wife and I recently bought a house on Kenmore Road, a couple of blocks behind your shop."

Jones continued cutting. "What's your name?"

"Chip Payne."

"I've been cutting hair in Lakeside for a long time, and I know a fair number of folks around here. There were some Payne's who lived here in Lakeside a long time ago. Might you be related to them?"

Chip answered, "Maybe. My dad and uncle grew up on Kent Street, and my grandmother worked at a gas station here on Lakeside Avenue during World War II and for a long time after that."

The barber abruptly stopped and looked up at the customer's reflection in the mirror. "You must be talking about Chris Payne. Is she your grandmother?"

"Yes," answered Chip excitedly.

"For real? You are Chris Payne's grandson?"

"Yes, I sure am. My dad is her son, Charles Payne," explained Chip.

"Well, I'll be. Chris Payne's grandson," the barber repeated. "If that don't beat all. I remember Chris very well. I was a customer at the station, and I tell you, that Chris - she was real foxy. A looker! Yes, she was, and a darned good mechanic too. Back when she was in her prime, those were the days. Lakeside hasn't been quite the same since then."

"Thank you," said Chip appreciatively.

"Well, you're certainly welcome, but there's no need to thank me. I'm just telling you how it was. Most people around here thought the world of your grandmother, and it's a pleasure to meet you."

As the barber continued cutting, he spun stories from his considerable memory, stories of Lakeside in the 1940s and '50s, and of things Chris had done during her career there. Chip reciprocated with his own stories of his "Granny Chris." He left the Lakeside Barbershop feeling that he belonged, that he was connected, that this was his home, even though he and his wife had just moved there.

There were other instances when her boys as grown men met people who knew Chris and offered kind and flattering words about her. Each of these was like a fresh chocolate chip cookie for the soul.

EPILOGUE

After serving in the Marine Corps Reserve, and with visions of flying, Gene elected to serve his active duty obligation in the air force, hoping the get to be a flight crewman. The Air Force had something else in mind for him, a specialty that he found less than appealing. When he was released from military service, he married the girl next door, Patricia Isbell. Well actually it was one door and a street between them. They eventually bought a house in Lakeside, where they raised their children.

Gene went to photography school and built a successful career in photo-lithography with William Byrd Press. When digital printing and photography came along, he went to school and learned four different computer programming languages and was responsible for converting the company's entire lithography operation from analog to digital. When he was moved up to management, he took college courses in business administration; all that, while maintaining his life-long hobby in ham radio, remaining and active in Hatcher Memorial Baptist Church, teaching, occasionally preaching, serving as a deacon and in the choir.

In retirement, Gene has pursued his hobby interest in photography; but a growing demand for his work pushed him into a second career, albeit a more leisurely one, as a professional portrait photographer. He is also a frequent contributing writer for the *Richmond Times Dispatch*. Gene and Pattie have three children-Brian, Kelly and Mark- and six grandchildren.

What became of Charlie? He is me, the one telling you this story. I enjoyed two years at home, just Chris and me. As a high school junior, I signed up for the Navy Reserve, attended drills and boot camp. In 1958, I took a training cruise and was seasick every time his ship passed the breakwaters going out, and stayed sick until it passed the breakwaters coming in. That navy experience reinforced my decision to go to college. It also persuaded me to take army ROTC and become an officer.

I graduated from Virginia Tech as a Dean's List student, with a commission in the army. All things considered, it was natural that I become a paratrooper jumping out of airplanes, and also natural that I become a lawyer. I entered law school at the University of Virginia but was called to active military duty before finishing. I served three-years as a paratrooper and was wounded in the Vietnam War. I left the service to return to law school, finishing in January, 1969. I spent the next 46 years in private practice in the Norfolk, Virginia Beach, Chesapeake area.

In retirement, I have redoubled my long-time interest in creative writing. Carolyn and I are active in a ministry helping military veterans and others overcome the effects of emotional shock and injury. We have three children – Kim, Chip and Steve. All three completed college, and our two boys completed graduate school, though neither became a lawyer. Between the three of them we have nine grandchildren and two great grandchildren, so far.

I think it fair to say that Chris's legacy to her descendants and the many people she helped throughout her life is returned to her as a fortune in blessings.

- - - - - - - - - The End - - - - - - - - -

78907469R00145

Made in the USA
Lexington, KY
15 January 2018